PIANO · VOCAL · GUITAR

THE NORMAN GIMBEL SONGBOOK

Photos © Bill Werts

ISBN 0-634-05888-6

HAL·LEONARD®
CORPORATION
7777 W. BLUEMOUND RD. P.O. BOX 13819 MILWAUKEE, WI 53213

Visit Hal Leonard Online at
www.halleonard.com

FOREWORD

This book brings together a body of work that belongs to our father. His songs have become well known over the years, and familiar to many an ear, but what this book truly represents to us is his absolute love of music, of melody, of the written word, of expression and voice, and his love for the magic that can happen when all of these are wed in song.

His lyrics have sophistication and sensitivity, as well as a wit, humor, and mood that touch us in so many ways. He has a gift and a style with words, and a choreography of language that is truly his own. We can feel him in his lyrics, as he is every word, and every word is him.

From left to right:
Hannah Gimbel,
Peter Gimbel,
Norman Gimbel,
Nelly Gimbel,
Anthony Gimbel

This book also represents to us our father's courage, spirit, and will to face the challenging and often solitary life of a writer, and to allow himself a vulnerability to create and express, and to not be afraid to search for truth. For this he is truly brave.

Norman Gimbel is a very special father and a very special writer, and how lucky we are to be a part of that.

Tony, Nelly, Peter, and Hannah Gimbel
November 20, 2003

BIOGRAPHICAL INFORMATION

Norman Gimbel is a native New Yorker who put his teaching degree from Columbia University into his safe and went downtown to pursue a career in songwriting instead. His first job in the music world was as an office boy for a music publisher in the famed Brill Building. There he met composer Larry Coleman and lyricist Joe Darion and with them wrote his first hit, "Ricochet Romance." Shortly after that, with composer-pianist Eddie Heywood, he wrote "Canadian Sunset."

His work caught the attention of Frank Loesser, who signed Gimbel as a contract writer. Under Loesser's guidance, he met composer Moose Charlap, with whom he wrote two Broadway musicals, *Whoop-Up* and *The Conquering Hero*.

In 1963 publisher Lou Levy introduced Gimbel to a young composer named Antonio Carlos Jobim. Gimbel would go on to write English versions of many of Jobim's songs, most notably the lyrics for "Meditation," "How Insensitive," "Áqua de Beber (Water to Drink)," "Song of the Sabiá" and "The Girl from Ipanema." Gimbel also wrote English lyrics for "Watch What Happens" and the Academy Award-nominated song "I Will Wait for You," both by Michel Legrand. For Jean "Toots" Thielemans he wrote the lyrics for his jazz waltz, "Bluesette."

In the fall of 1967, Gimbel moved to Hollywood where he became active in film and television. Among the composers he worked with there were Lalo Shifrin, Maurice Jarre, Henry Mancini, Robert Folk, David Shire, Peter Matz, and his principal collaborator, Charles Fox.

Gimbel had some of his biggest successes with Fox, with whom he wrote TV title songs to "Happy Days," "Laverne and Shirley," "Wonder Woman," "Angie" and "Paper Chase." Their collaboration also included "I Got a Name" for the 1973 film *The Last American Hero*. This became a Top 10 hit for Jim Croce. Fox and Gimbel also gave us "Killing Me Softly with His Song," which won the Grammy Award for Song of the Year in 1973 and is currently ranked No. 11 on BMI's list of "Top 100 Songs." Also with Fox he wrote "Richard's Window" for the film *The Jill Kinmont Story*. This received an Academy Award Nomination in 1975. They received another Academy Award nomination in 1978 for "Ready to Take a Chance Again," from the film *Foul Play*. In collaboration with composer David Shire, for the 1979 film *Norma Rae*, he wrote "It Goes Like It Goes," the song that won Gimbel an Academy Award for Best Original Song.

Norman Gimbel's songs have appeared in over seventy motion picture and television shows. Gimbel was inducted into the Songwriters Hall of Fame in 1984.

CONTENTS
(Alphabetical)

CONTENTS
(Chronological)

Norman Gimbel inducted into the
Songwriters Hall of Fame in 1984.
From left to right: daughter of inductee
Maceo Pinkard, and fellow inductees
Henry Mancini, George Weiss, Gimbel,
Richard Adler, Benny Benjamin,
Pinkard, Neil Diamond
and Sammy Cahn.

Norman Gimbel and Charles Fox
receive the Grammy Award for
Song of the Year in 1973.
From left to right: Gimbel, Fox,
Lily Tomlin, Roberta Flack
and Isaac Hayes.

Norman Gimbel and
David Shire win the
Academy Award for
Best Original Song in 1979.
From left to right: Presenter
Olivia Newton-John, Shire,
Gimbel and Presenter
Gene Kelly.

AM I FEELING LOVE

from the Miramax Film ARABIAN KNIGHT

Words by NORMAN GIMBEL
Music by ROBERT FOLK

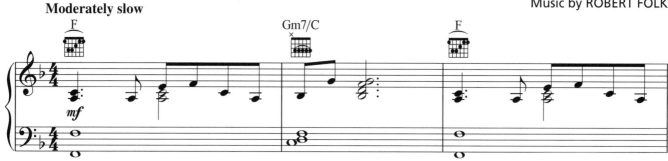

I close my eyes and see { his } eyes
                        { her }

so soft and warm and bright.   I dream a-wake of

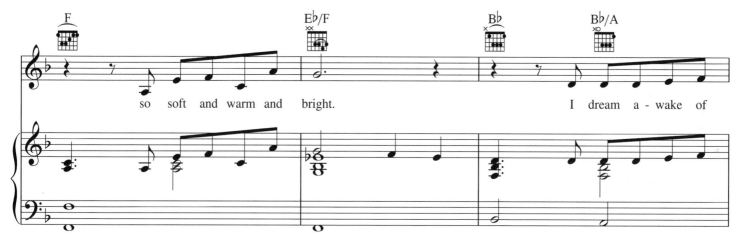

hold - ing { her }   all through an end - less night.
          { him }

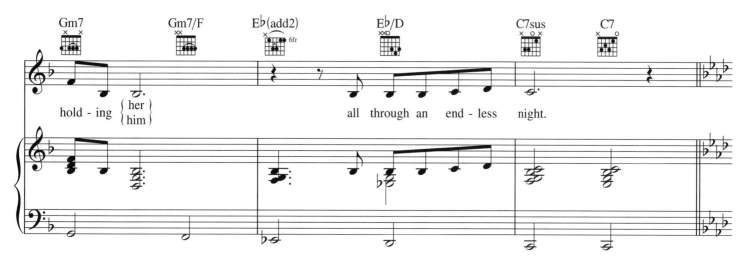

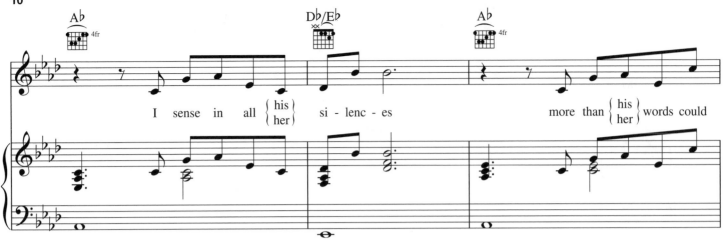

I sense in all {his} {her} si- lenc- es more than {his} {her} words could

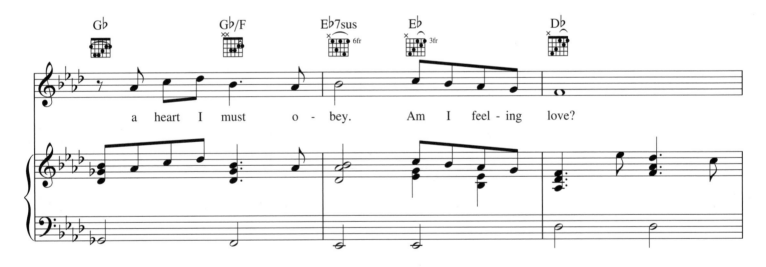

say. I'm just a {boy} {girl} ruled by my heart,

a heart I must o- bey. Am I feel- ing love?

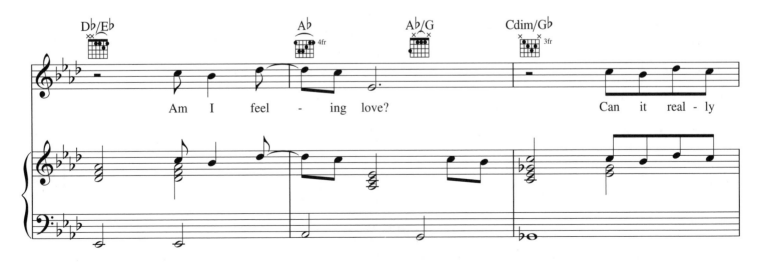

Am I feel- ing love? Can it real- ly

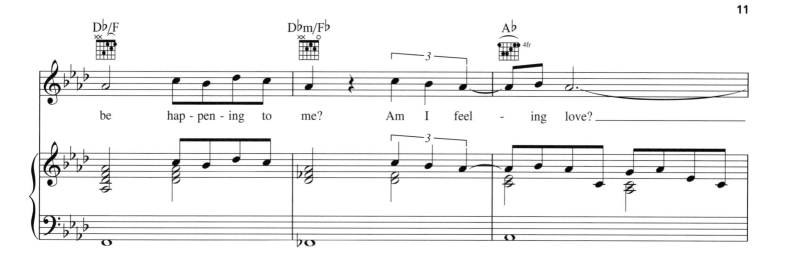

be hap-pen-ing to me? Am I feel - ing love? _____

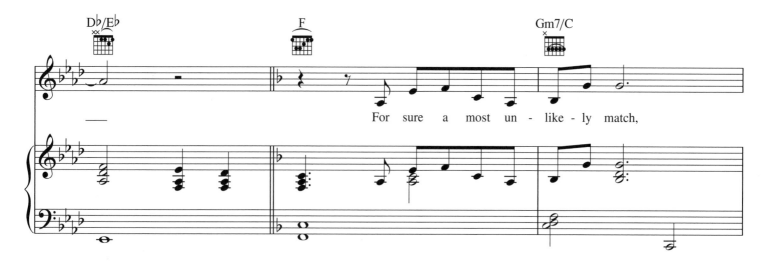

_____ For sure a most un - like - ly match,

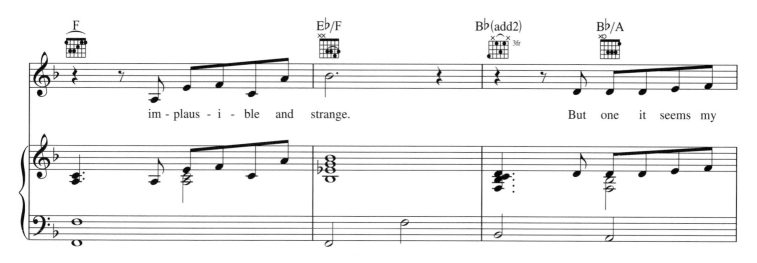

im - plaus - i - ble and strange. But one it seems my

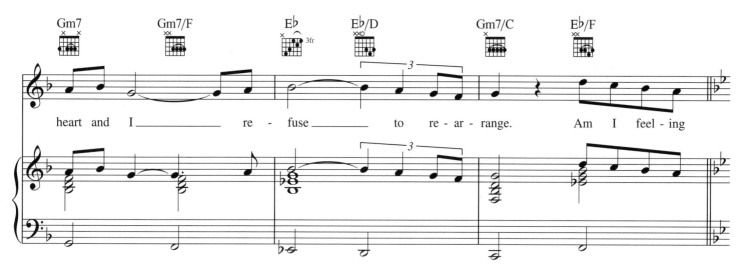

heart and I _____ re - fuse _____ to re - ar - range. Am I feel - ing

love? Am I feel - ing love? _____ Can it real - ly

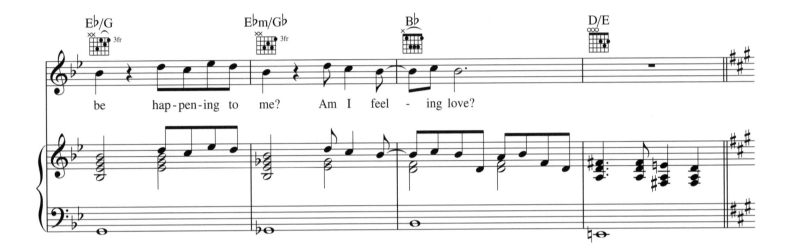

be hap - pen - ing to me? Am I feel - ing love?

I think I feel { he'd / she'd } be there ___ for me. ___ I feel I think

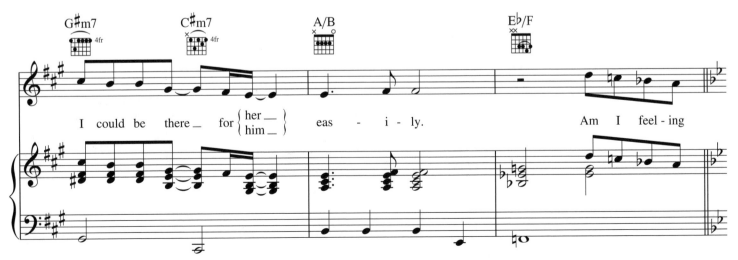

I could be there ___ for { her ___ / him ___ } eas - i - ly. Am I feel - ing

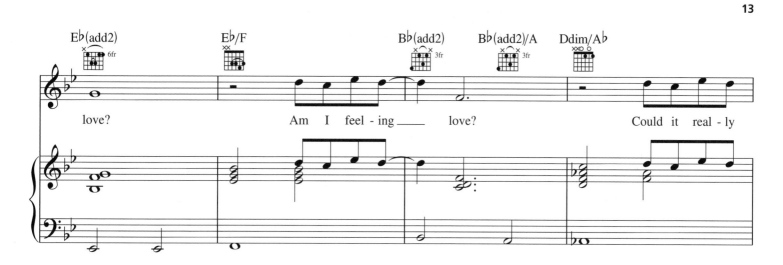

love?   Am I feel - ing ___ love?   Could it real - ly

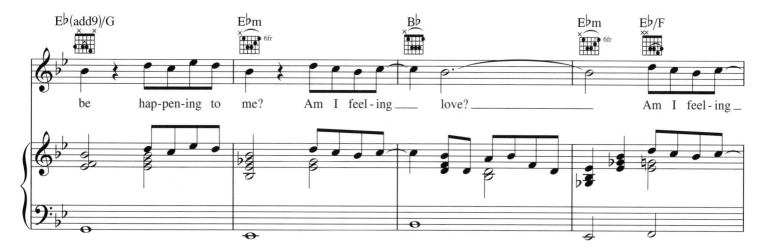

be   hap-pen-ing to   me?   Am I feel - ing ___ love? ___   Am I feel - ing __

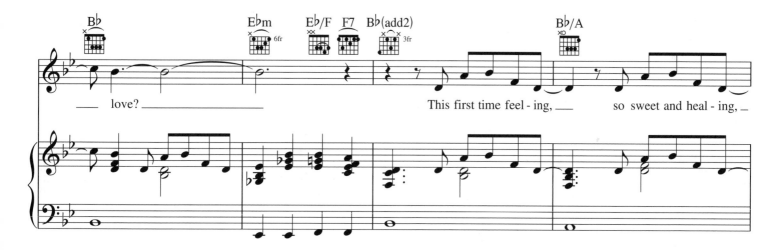

___ love? ___   This first time feel - ing, ___   so sweet and heal - ing, __

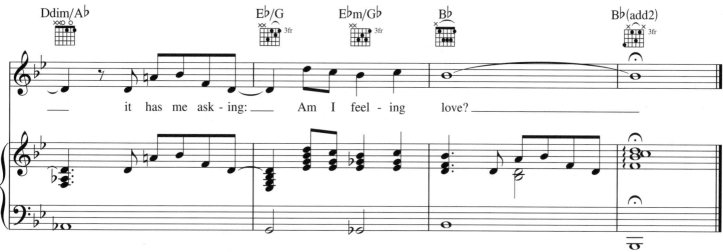

___   it   has me ask - ing: ___   Am I feel - ing   love? ___

ÁGUA DE BEBER
(Water to Drink)

English Words by NORMAN GIMBEL
Portuguese Words by VINICIUS DE MORAES
Music by ANTONIO CARLOS JOBIM

Lyrics:
Your love ___ is rain, ___ ___ my heart ___ the flow - er. ___
on dis - tant des - erts. ___

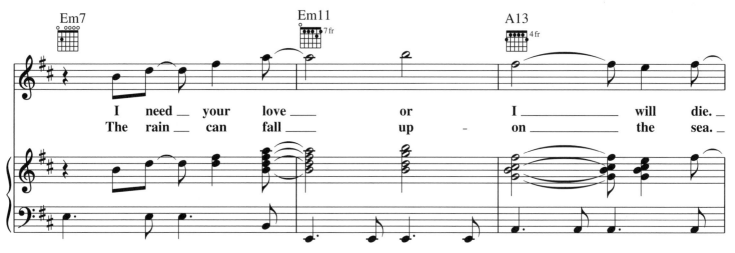

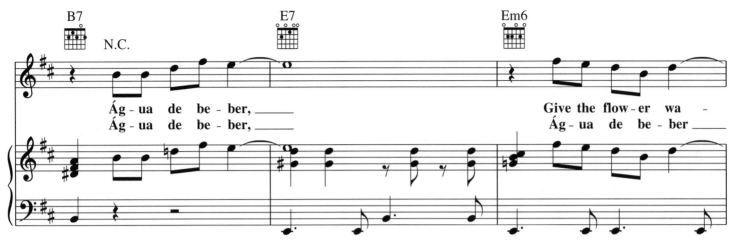

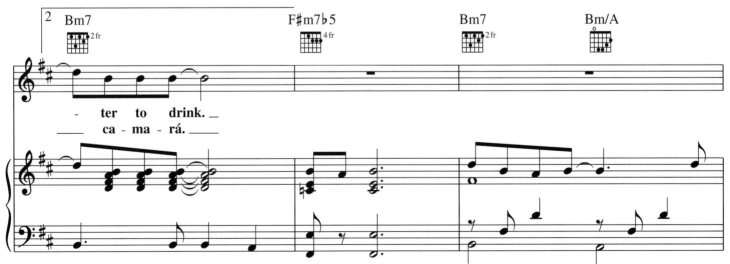

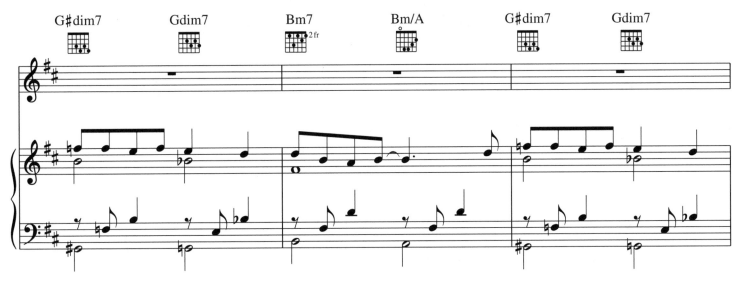

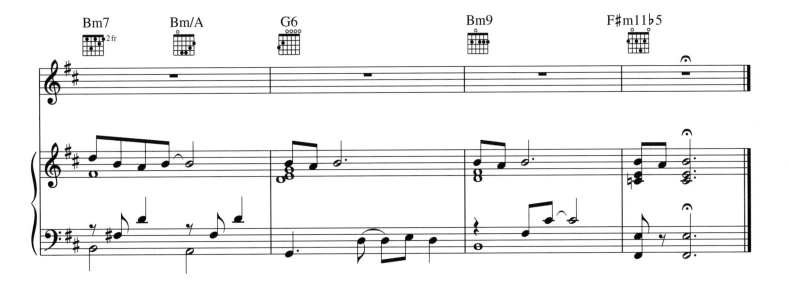

Portuguese Lyrics

Eu quis amar Mas tive medo
E quis salvar meu coração
Mas o amor sabe um segredo
O medo pode matar o seu coração

Água de beber
Água de beber camará
Água de beber
Água de beber camará

Eu nunca fiz coisa tão certa
Entrei pra escola do perdão
A minha casa vive aberta
Abre todas as portas do coração

Água de beber...

Eu sempre tive uma certeza
Que só me deu desilusão
É que o amor É uma tristeza
Muita mágoa demais para um coração

Água de beber...

ALWAYS THERE

Walt Disney Pictures presents LADY & THE TRAMP II: SCAMP'S ADVENTURE

Words and Music by NORMAN GIMBEL
and MELISSA MANCHESTER

Moderately slow, expressively

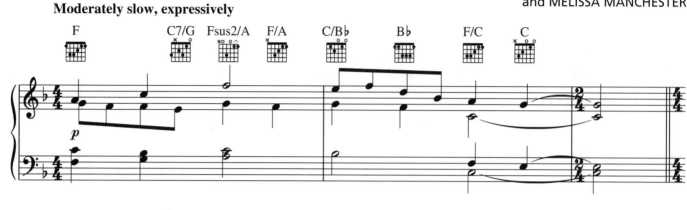

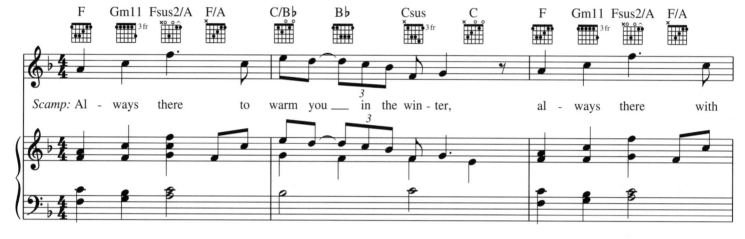

Scamp: Al - ways there to warm you ___ in the win - ter, al - ways there with

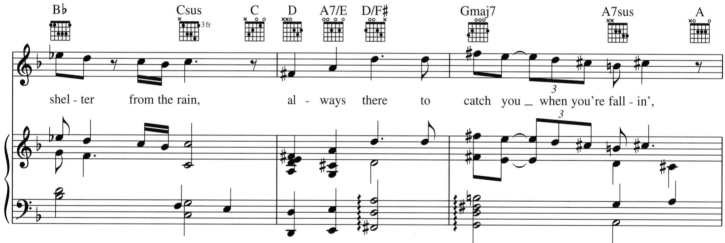

shel - ter from the rain, al - ways there to catch you ___ when you're fall - in',

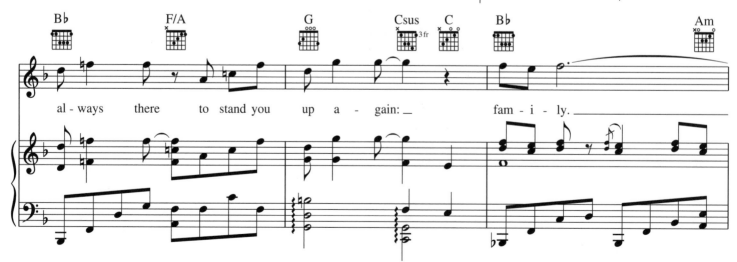

al - ways there to stand you up a - gain: ___ fam - i - ly. ___

*Female vocal written one octave higher than sung.

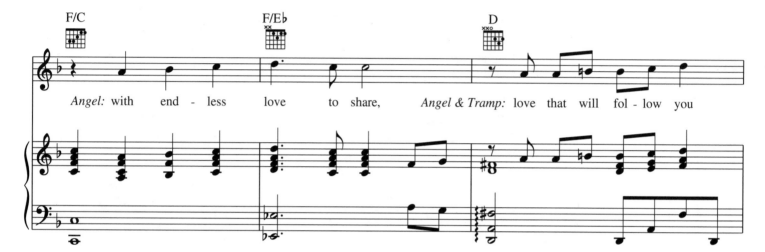

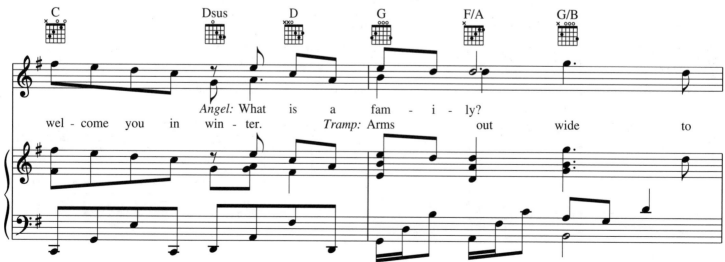

AMAZING

English Words by NORMAN GIMBEL
French Words by EDDY MARNAY
Music by EMILE STERN

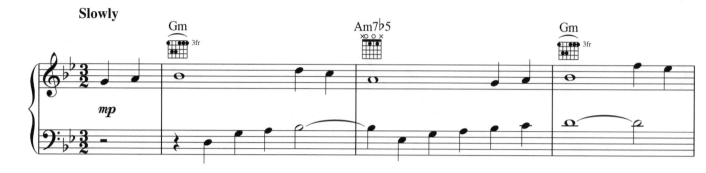

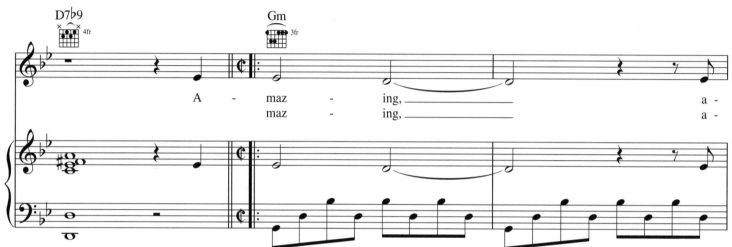

A - maz - ing, _____ a -
maz - ing, _____ a -

maz - ing, _____ it all ___ seems ___
maz - ing, _____ your mag - ic ___

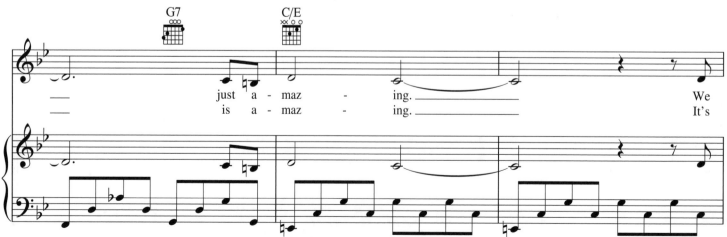

just a - maz - ing. _____ We
is a - maz - ing. _____ It's

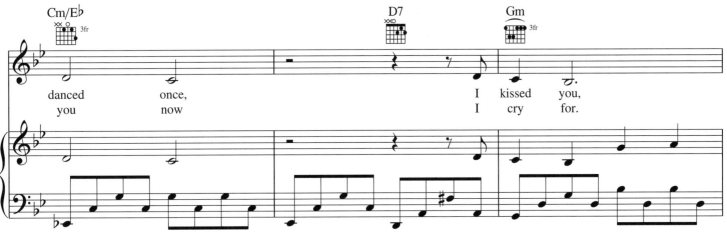

danced   once,   I   kissed   you,
you   now   I   cry   for.

and   now   I   can't   re -
It's   you   that   I   would

sist   you.
die   for.   A -   Who   knew   one

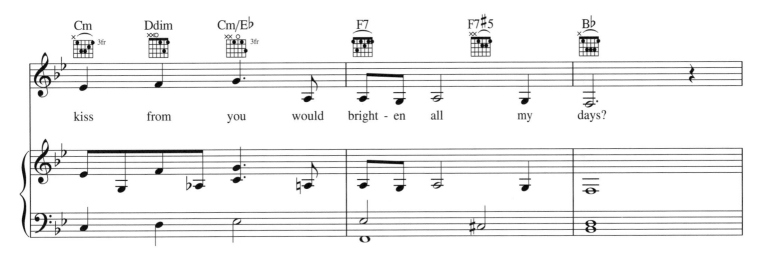

kiss   from   you   would   bright - en   all   my   days?

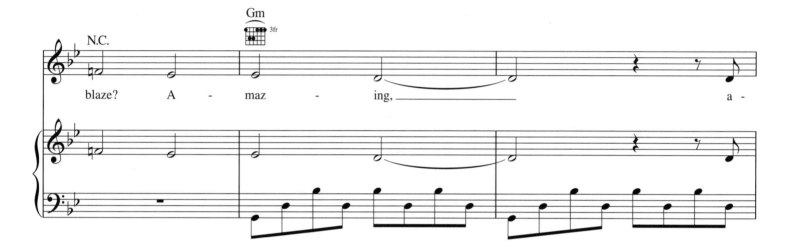

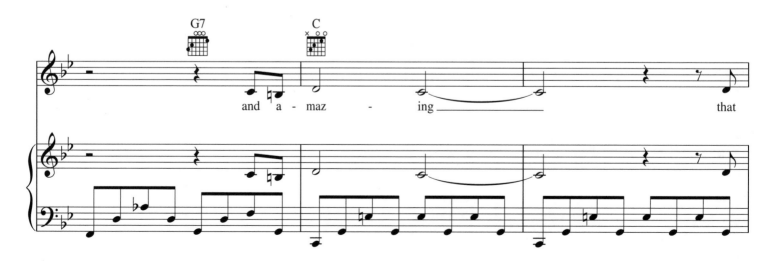

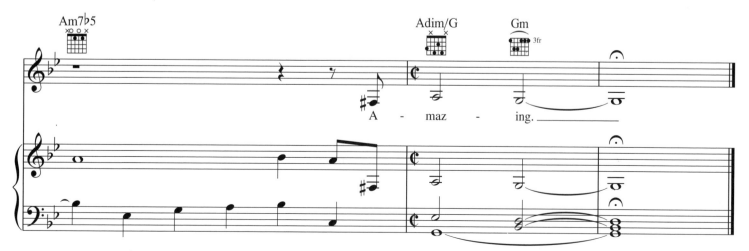

BITS AND PIECES
from the 20th Century Fox Film THE STUNT MAN

Music by DOMINIC FRONTIERE
Words by NORMAN GIMBEL

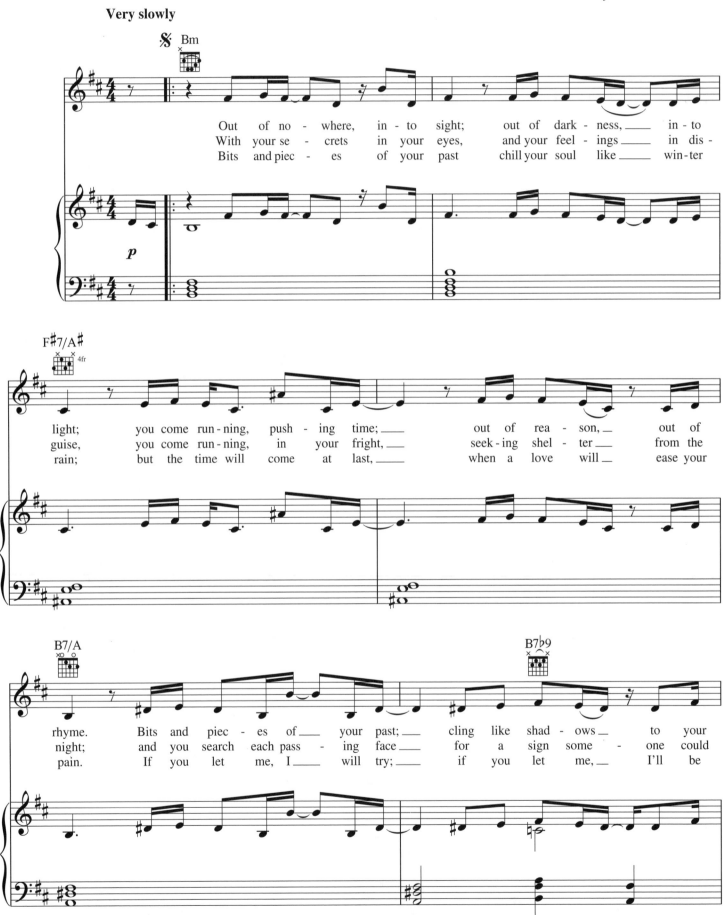

BLUESETTE

Words by NORMAN GIMBEL
Music by JEAN THIELEMANS

Poor lit - tle, sad lit - tle blue Blues - ette.
Long as there's love in your heart to share,

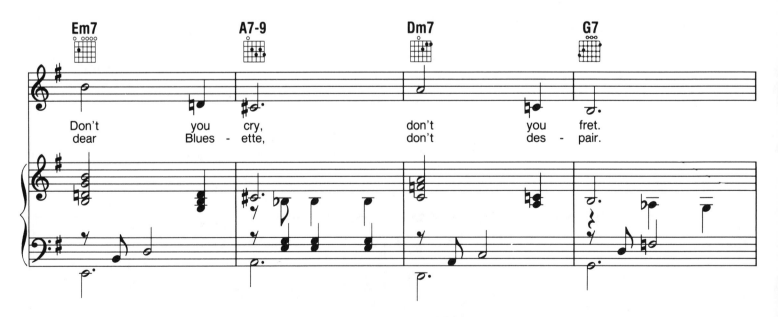

Don't you cry, don't you fret.
dear Blues - ette, don't des - pair.

CANADIAN SUNSET

Words by NORMAN GIMBEL
Music by EDDIE HEYWOOD

Moderately, with a good beat

Once, _____ I was a - lone
Cold, _____ cold was the wind

So, _____ lone - ly and then, you came, _____
Warm, _____ warm were your lips, out there _____

_____ out of no - where, _____ like the sun _____ up from the
_____ on that ski trail _____ where your kiss, _____ filled me with

COME WITH ME NOW

Theme from LIFESTYLES OF THE RICH & FAMOUS

Music by BILL CONTI
Words by NORMAN GIMBEL

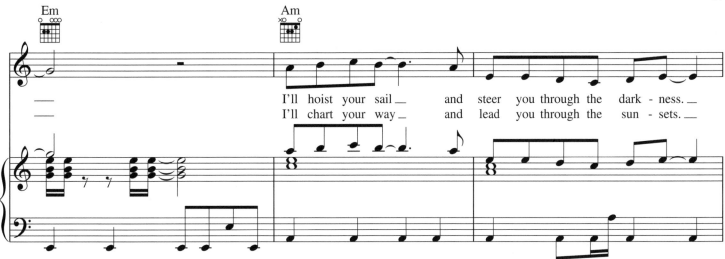

I'll hoist your sail __ and steer you through the dark - ness. __
I'll chart your way __ and lead you through the sun - sets. __

I'll be your friend __ and take you safe - ly through. _____
I'll be your friend __ and speed you safe - ly there. _____

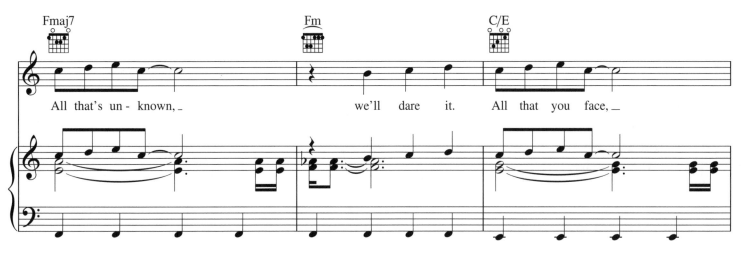

All that's un - known, _ we'll dare it. All that you face, _

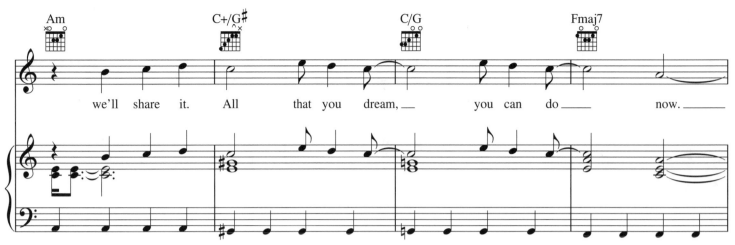

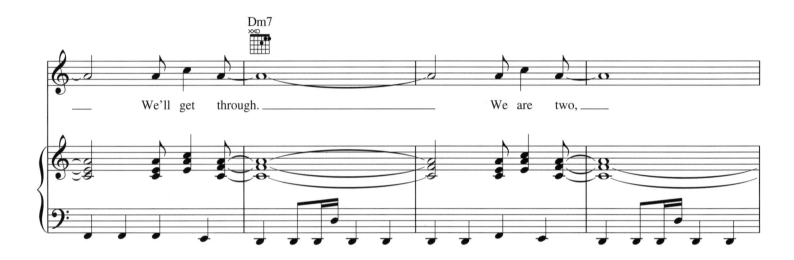

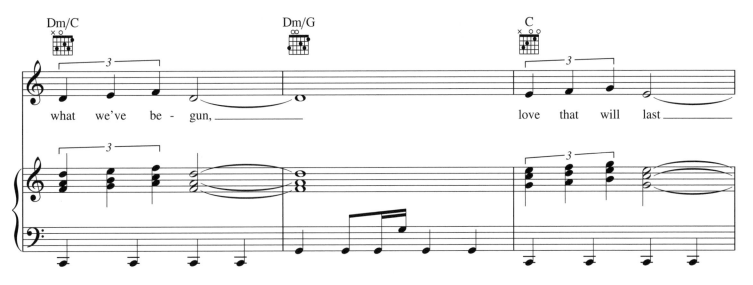

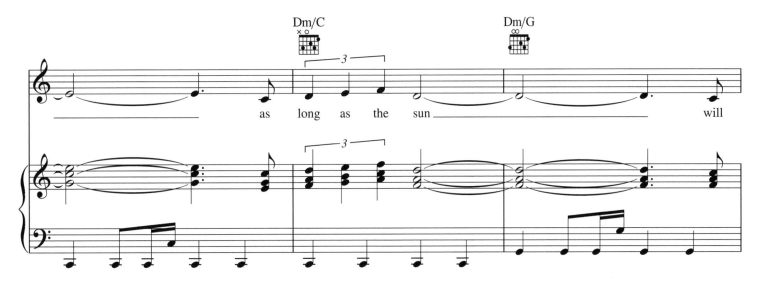

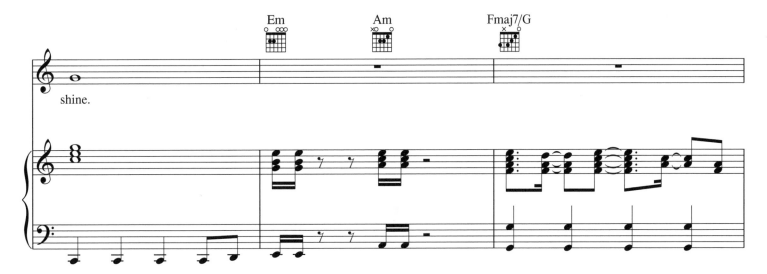

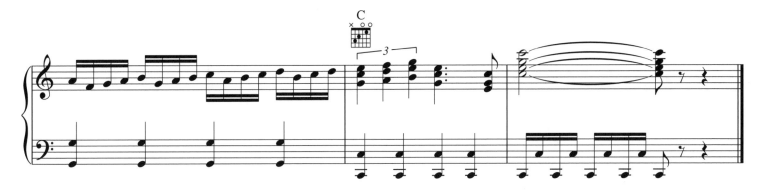

DIFFERENT

from the Universal Film PUFNSTUF

Music by CHARLES FOX
Words by NORMAN GIMBEL

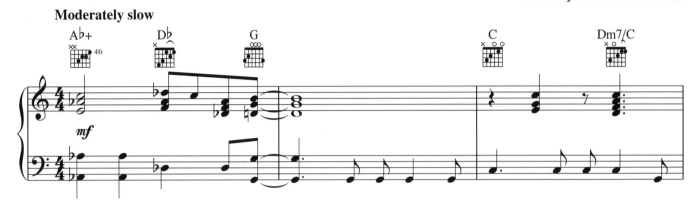

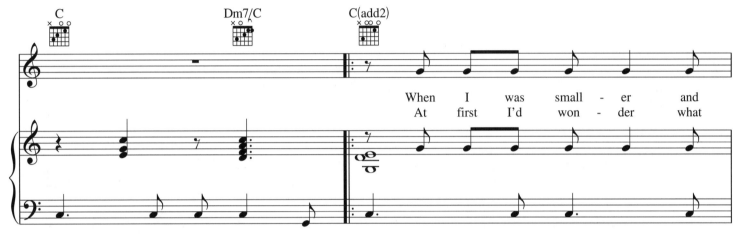

*Alternate lyric: feeling

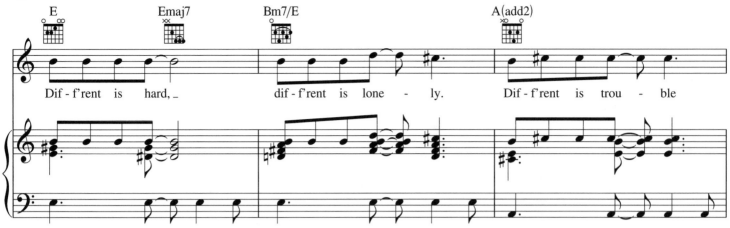

Dif - f'rent is hard, _ dif - f'rent is lone - ly. Dif - f'rent is trou - ble

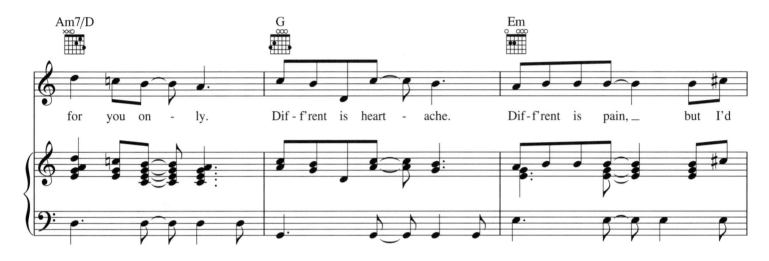

for you on - ly. Dif - f'rent is heart - ache. Dif - f'rent is pain, _ but I'd

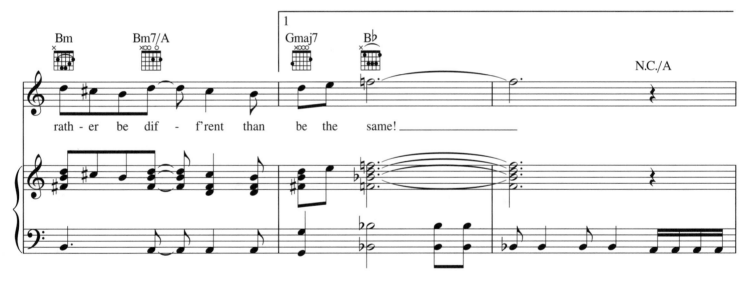

rath - er be dif - f'rent than be the same! _

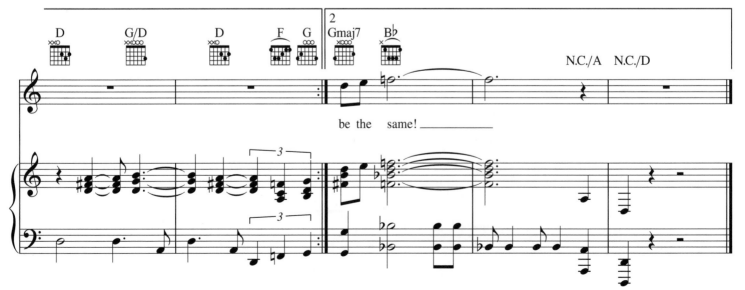

be the same! _

FLATTERY

from the Broadway Musical WHOOP-UP

Words by NORMAN GIMBEL
Music by MORRIS CHARLAP

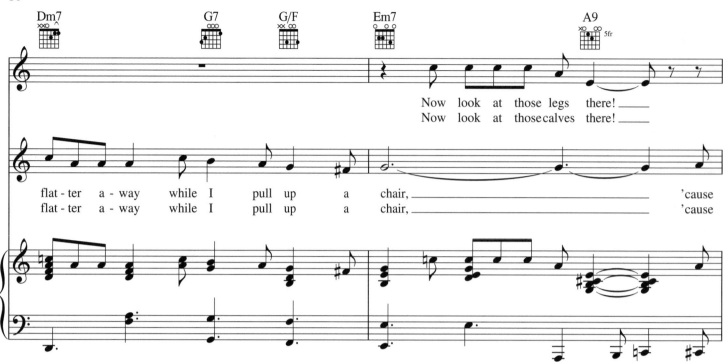

Now look at those legs there! _____
Now look at those calves there! _____

flat - ter a - way while I pull up a chair, _____ 'cause
flat - ter a - way while I pull up a chair, _____ 'cause

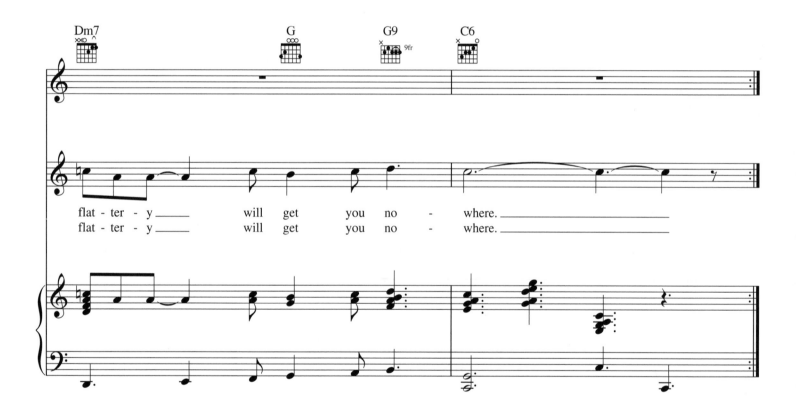

flat - ter - y _____ will get you no - where. _____
flat - ter - y _____ will get you no - where. _____

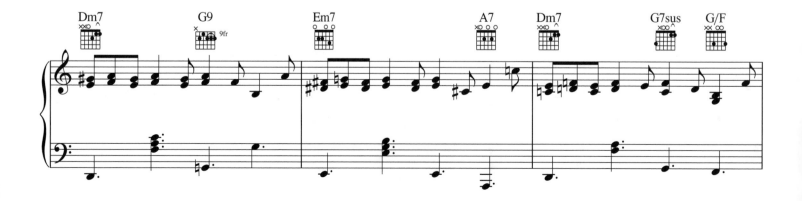

DIFFERENT WORLDS
Theme from the Paramount Television Series ANGIE

Words NORMAN GIMBEL
Music by CHARLES FOX

Moderately, with a strong beat

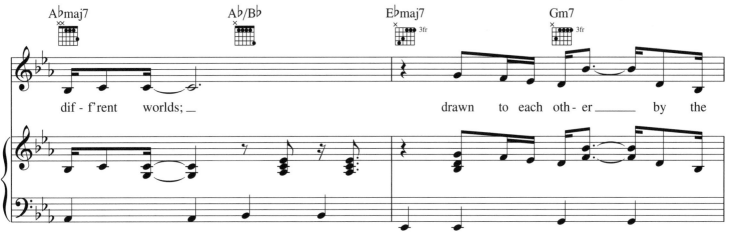

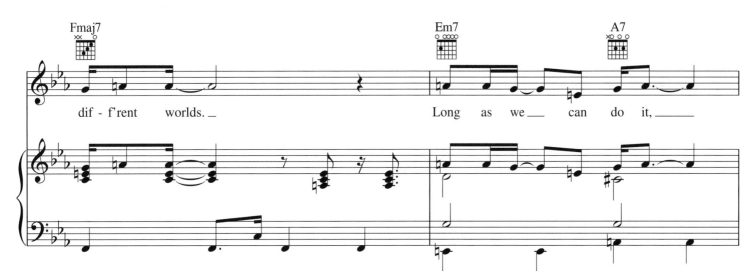

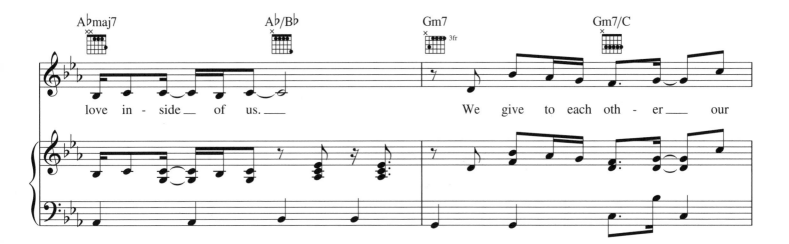

time _ flow, _ let the love grow, _ let the rain _ show'r, _ let the rose _

_ flow'r. _ Love, it seeks; _ love, it finds; _

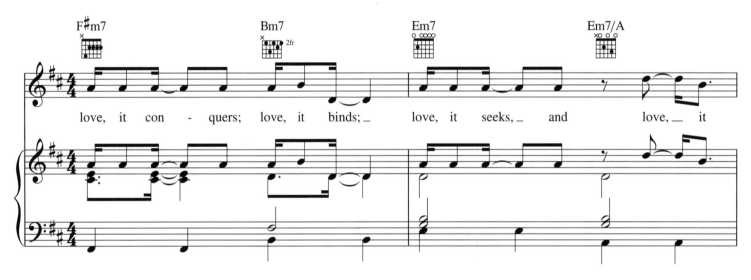

love, it con - quers; love, it binds; _ love, it seeks, _ and love, _ it

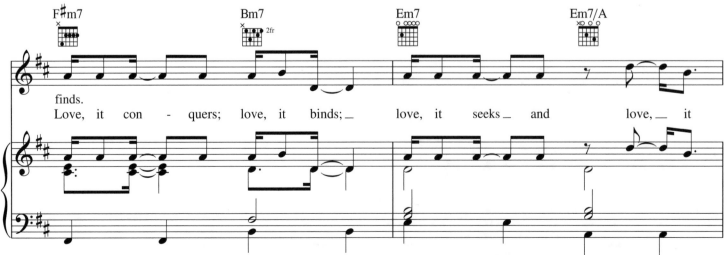

finds.
Love, it con - quers; love, it binds; _ love, it seeks _ and love, _ it

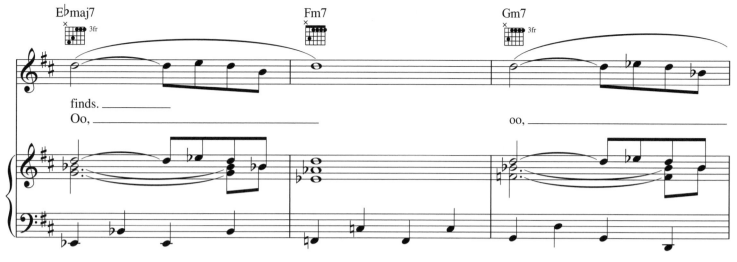

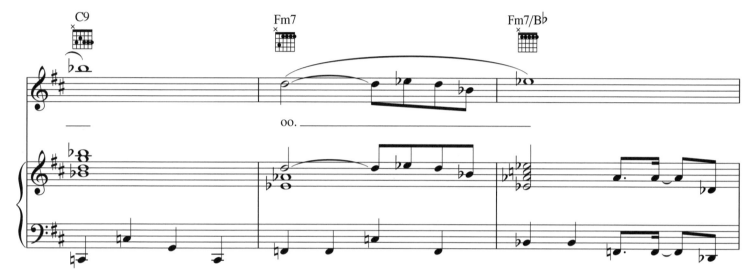

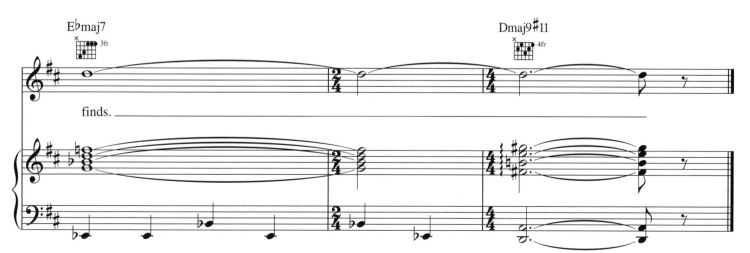

GIRL
from the Paramount Film STAR SPANGLED GIRL

Words by NORMAN GIMBEL
Music by CHARLES FOX

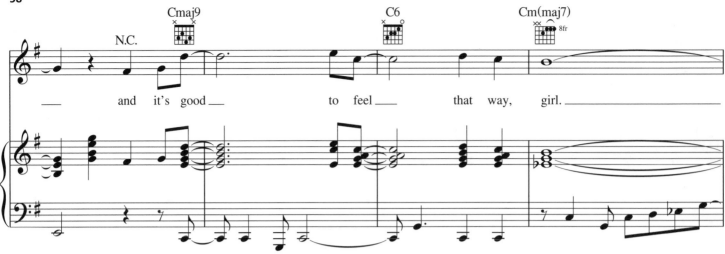

and it's good ____ to feel ____ that way, girl. ____

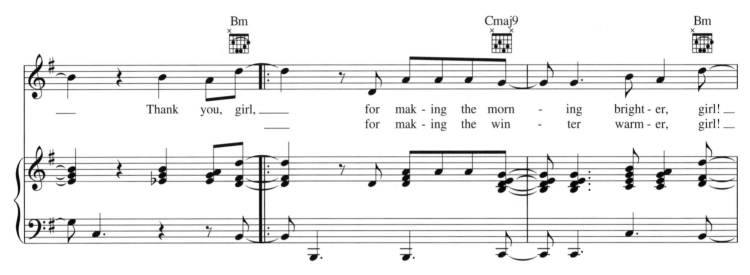

Thank you, girl, ____ for mak - ing the morn - ing bright - er, girl! ____
____ for mak - ing the win - ter warm - er, girl! ____

For mak - ing the night - time nic - er, girl! ____ For mak - ing a bet -
For mak - ing the mu - sic soft - er, girl! ____ For mak - ing a bet -

Repeat and Fade

- ter world ____ for me. ____ Thank you, girl, ____
- ter world ____ for me. ____ Thank you, girl, ____

THE GIRL FROM IPANEMA
(Garôta de Ipanema)

Music by ANTONIO CARLOS JOBIM
English Words by NORMAN GIMBEL
Original Words by VINICIUS DE MORAES

Bossa Nova

Tall and tan and young___ and {love - ly, the girl___} from I - pa - ne-
                                {hand - some, the boy___}

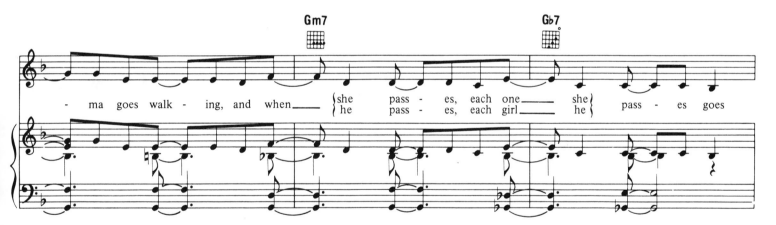

- ma goes walk - ing, and when___ {she pass - es, each one___ she} pass - es goes
                                   {he pass - es, each girl___ he}

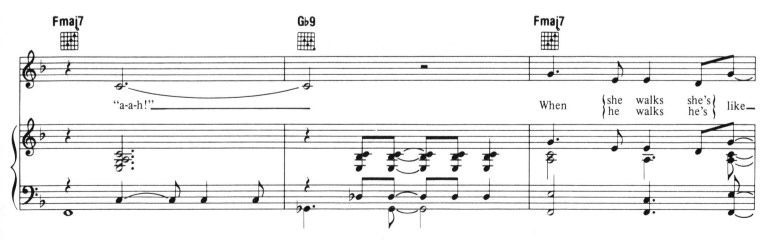

"a-a-h!"___ When {she walks she's} like___
                 {he walks he's}

GIRL IN THE MOON

Words by NORMAN GIMBEL
Music by NELLY RANSOM GIMBEL

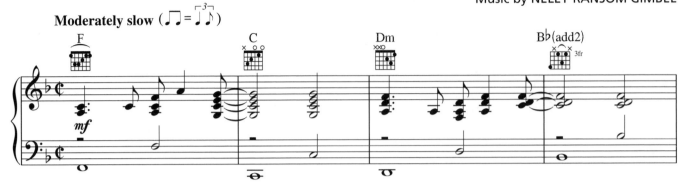

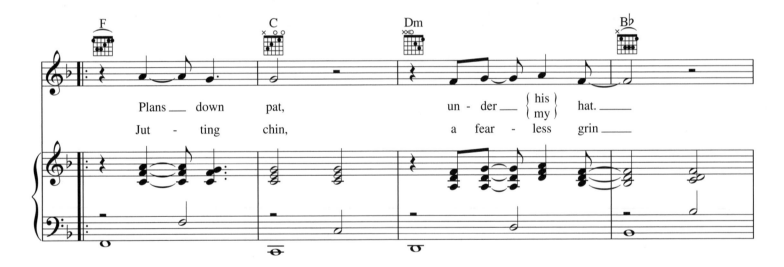

Plans ___ down pat,   un - der ___ {his}{my} hat. ___

Jut - ting chin,   a fear - less grin ___

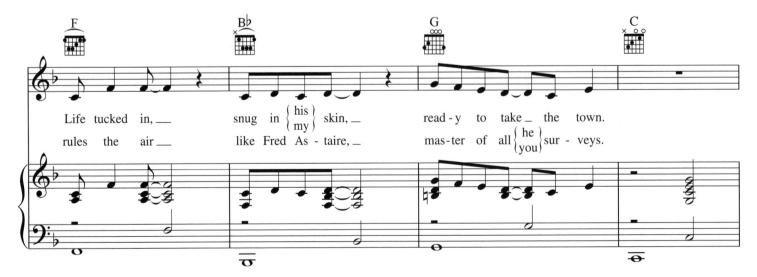

Life tucked in, ___   snug in {his}{my} skin, ___   read - y to take ___ the town.

rules the air ___   like Fred As - taire, ___   mas - ter of all {he}{you} sur - veys.

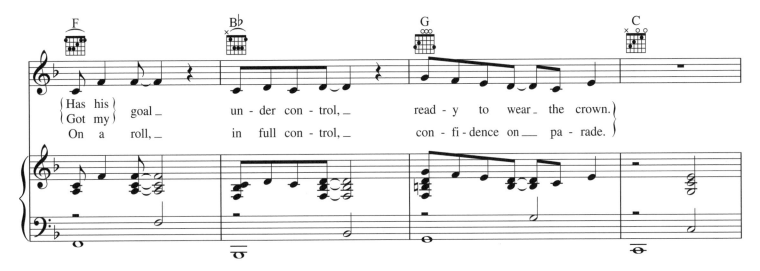

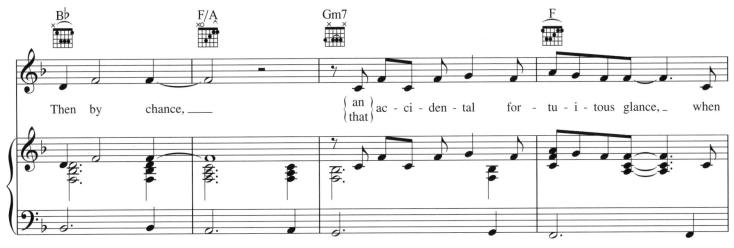

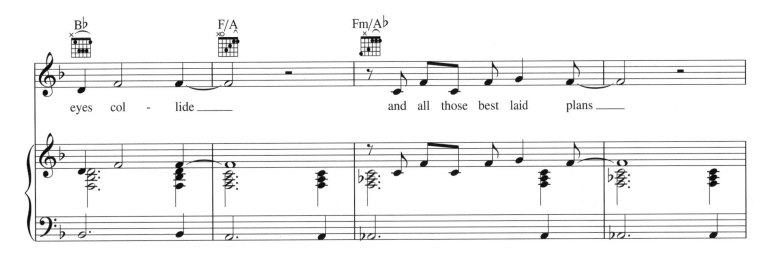

drift out with the tide. Etched in glass _ and paint-ed on clouds, _ her

grin-ning face _ is ev - 'ry-where. Girl in the moon, _

girl in the moon. _ She's in {his my} head _ and start-ing to spread _ her

voo-doo moon-light ev - 'ry-where. _ Girl in the moon, _

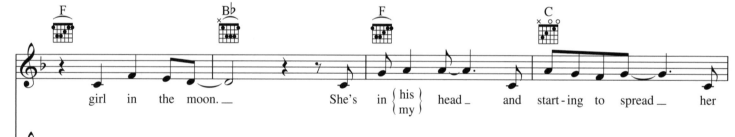

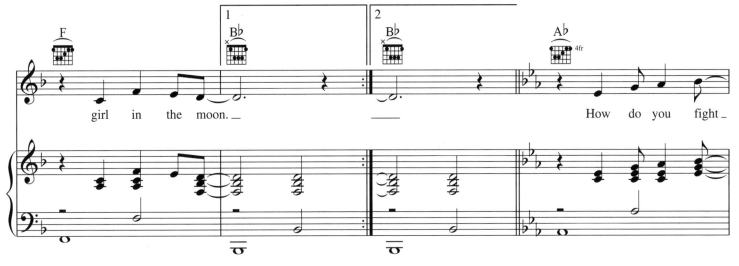

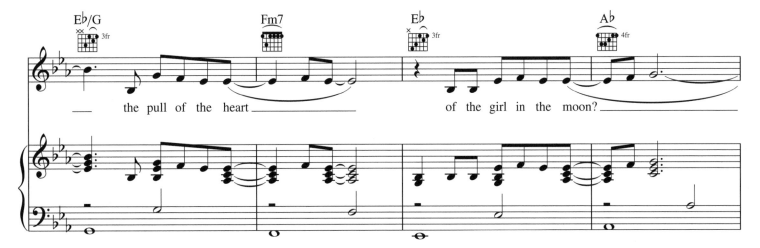

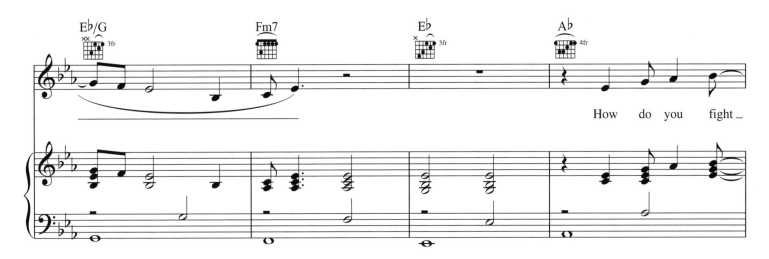

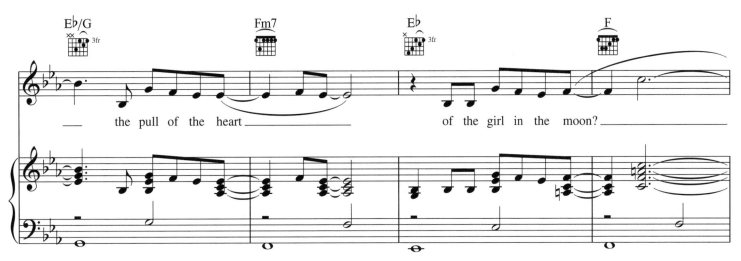

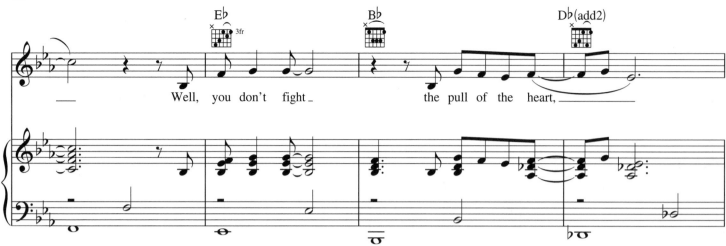

Well, you don't fight _ the pull of the heart, _____ the

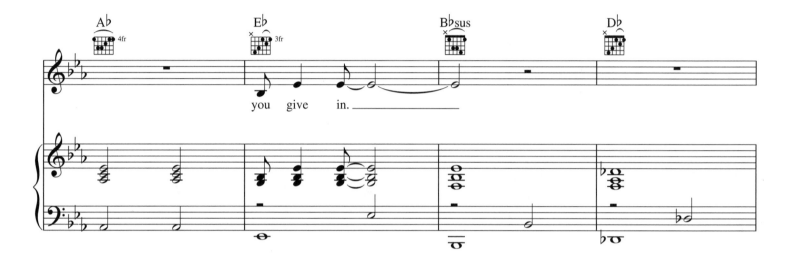

you give in. _____

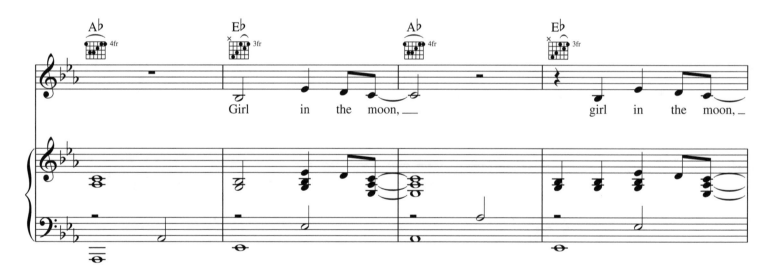

Girl in the moon, __ girl in the moon, _

_ girl in the moon. _____

GOOD FRIEND

from the Paramount Film MEATBALLS

Words by NORMAN GIMBEL
Music by ELMER BERNSTEIN

Moderately

Do do do ___ do ah, do do do ___ do ah, do do do ___ do ah,

do do do ___ do ah. If you let ___ me, _____ I could be your

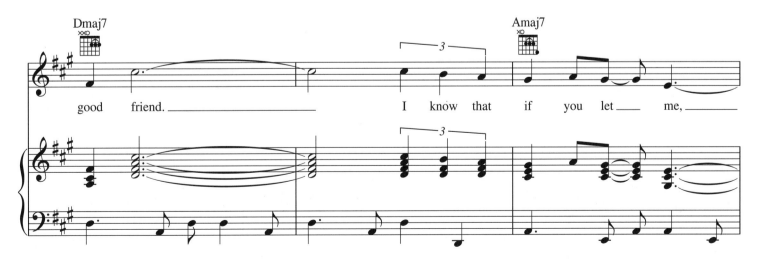

good friend. _____ I know that if you let ___ me, _____

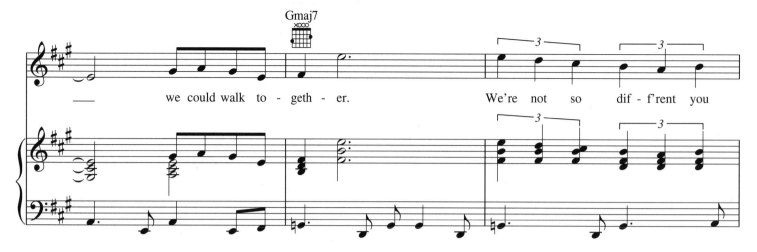

we could walk to - geth - er. We're not so dif - f'rent you

know, though we may have dif - f'rent dreams. ____

When they fall a - part, ____ we hurt the

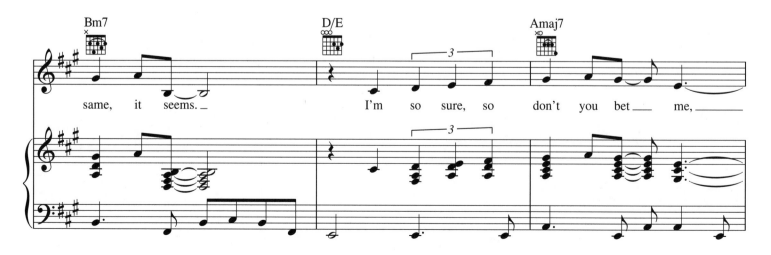

same, it seems. ____ I'm so sure, so don't you bet ____ me, ____

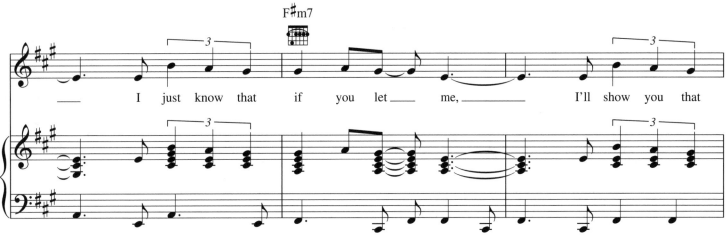

I just know that if you let ___ me, ____ I'll show you that

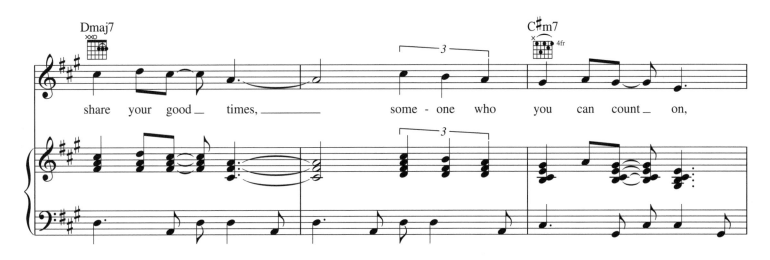

I could be ___ your good friend. Some-one to

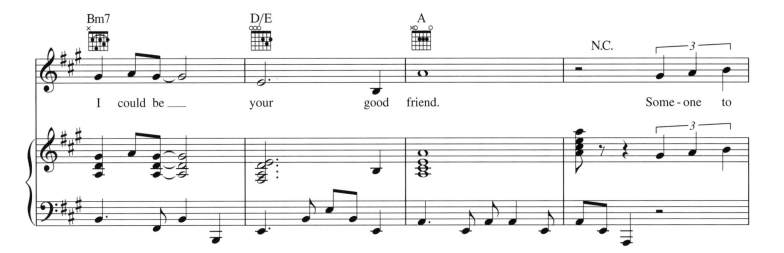

share your good ___ times, ___ some-one who you can count ___ on,

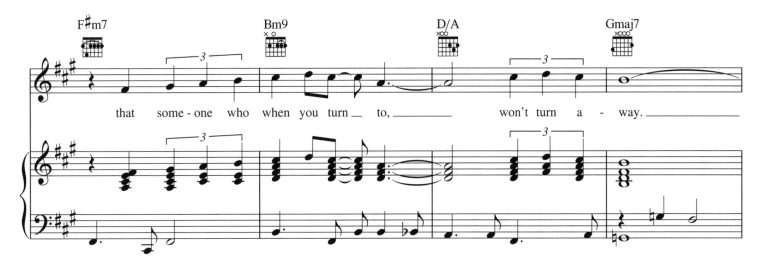

that some-one who when you turn ___ to, ___ won't turn a-way. ___

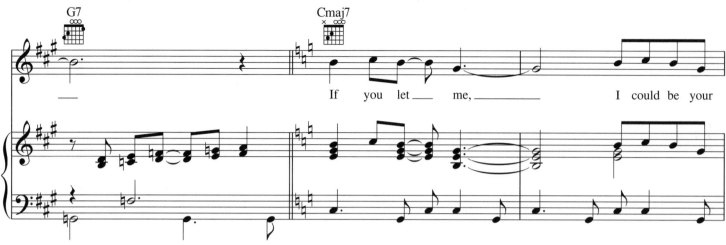

If you let ___ me, ___ I could be your

good friend. ___ I know that if you let ___ me, ___ we could walk to -

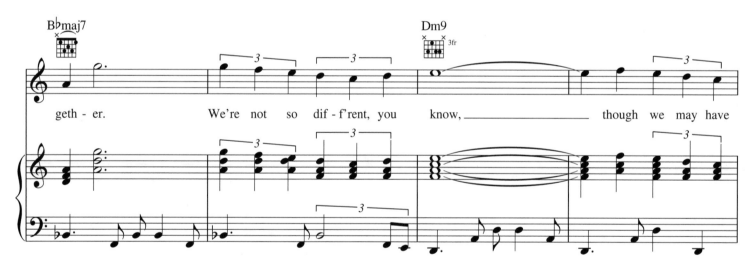

geth - er. We're not so dif - f'rent, you know, ___ though we may have

dif - f'rent dreams. ___ When they fall a - part, ___ we hurt the

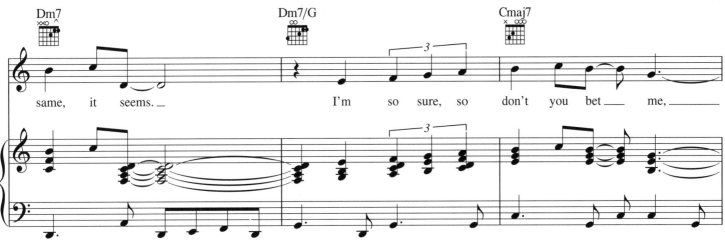

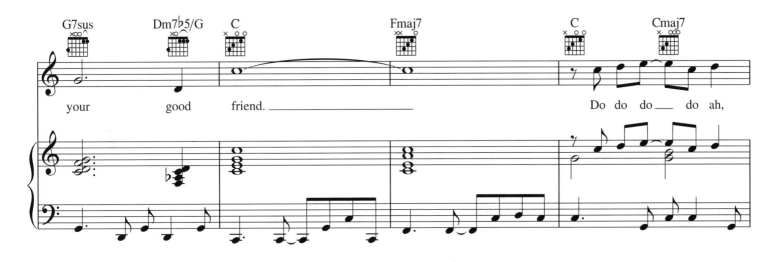

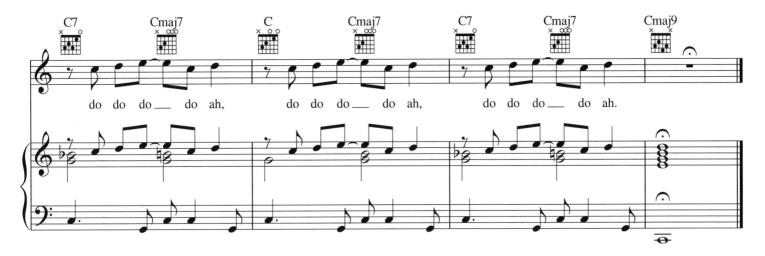

HAPPY DAYS
Theme from the Paramount Television Series HAPPY DAYS

Words by NORMAN GIMBEL
Music by CHARLES FOX

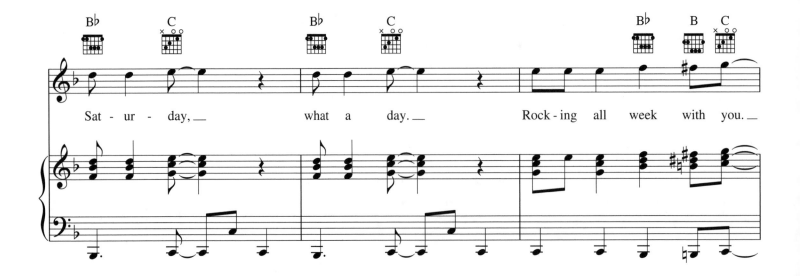

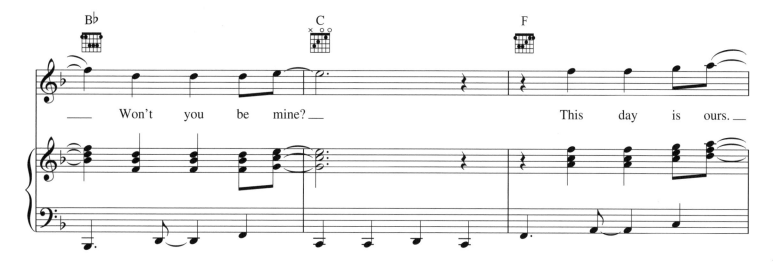

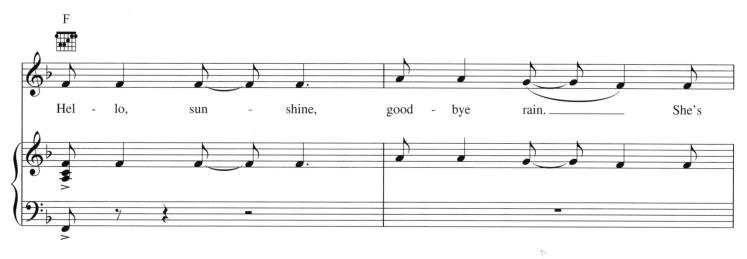

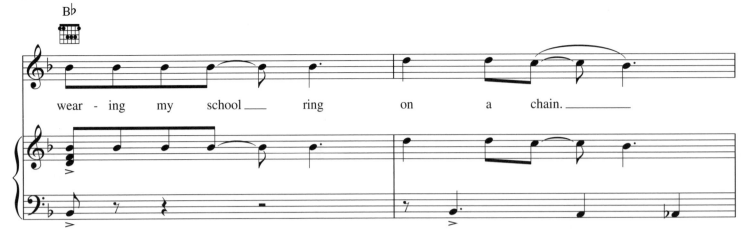

wear - ing my school ___ ring on a chain. ___

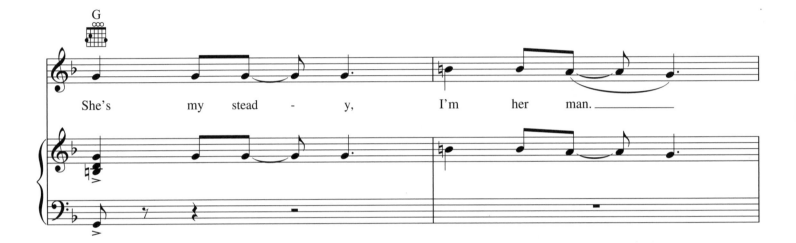

She's my stead - y, I'm her man. ___

I'm gon - na love her all ___ I can. ___ This day is ours. ___

Won't you be mine? ___

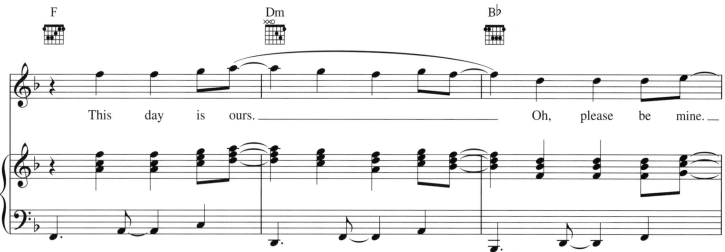

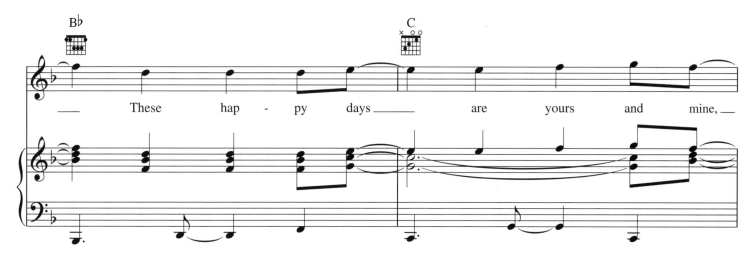

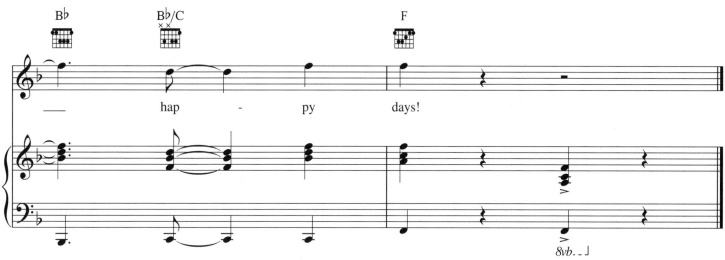

HOW INSENSITIVE
(Insensatez)

Music by ANTONIO CARLOS JOBIM
Original Words by VINICIUS DE MORAES
English Words by NORMAN GIMBEL

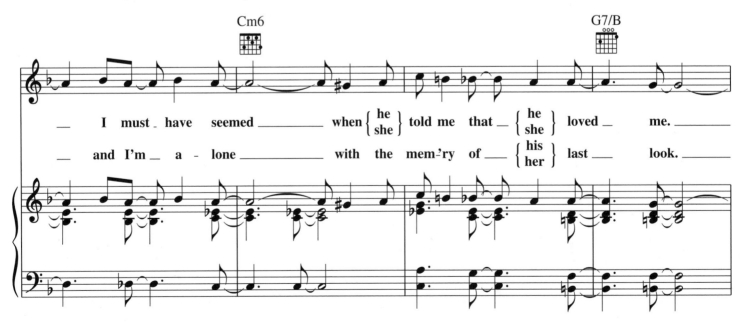

How un-moved and cold
Vague and drawn and sad,

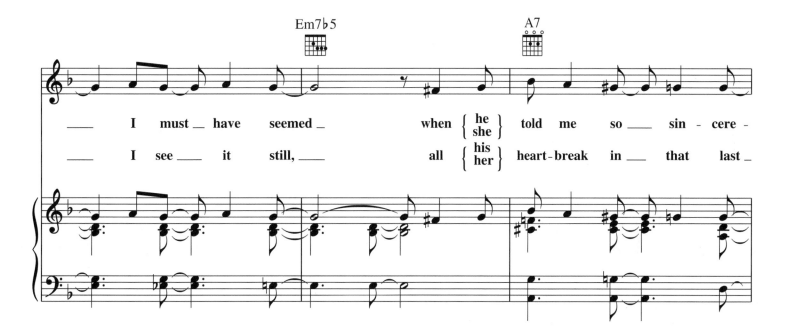

I must have seemed when {he / she} told me so sin-cere-
I see it still, all {his / her} heart-break in that last

-ly. Why,
look. How,

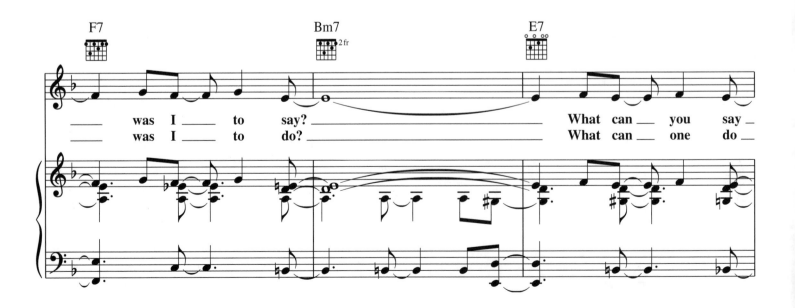

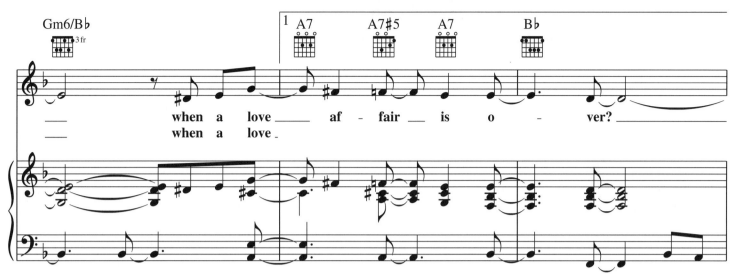

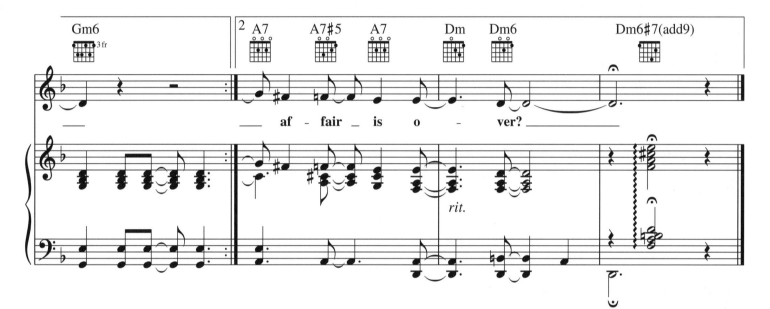

Portuguese Lyrics

A insensatez
Que você fez
Coração mais sem cuidado
Fez chorar de dôr
O seu amôr
Um amôr tão delicado
Ah! Porque você
Foi fraco assim
Assim tão desalmado
Ah! Meu coração
Que nunca amou
Não merece ser amado
Vai meu coração
Ouve a razão
Usa só sinceridade
Quem semeia vento
Diz a razão
Colhe tempestade
Vai meu coração
Pede perdão
Perdão apaixonado
Vai porque
Quem não
Pede perdão
Não é nunca perdoado.

I GOT A NAME

from the 20th Century Fox Film LAST AMERICAN HERO

Words by NORMAN GIMBEL
Music by CHARLES FOX

toad, I've got a name;_____ I've got a name,_____
cry, I've got a song;_____ I've got a song,_____
(Instrumental) _____
me, I've got a dream;_____ I've got a dream.

and I car - ry it with_____ me like my
and I car - ry it with_____ me and I
(Instrumental) _____
Oh, I know I could share_____ it if you'd

dad - dy did,_____ but I'm liv - ing the dream_____
sing it loud;_____ if it gets me no where,_____
(Instrumental) _____
want me to;_____ if you're go - in' my_____ way,_____

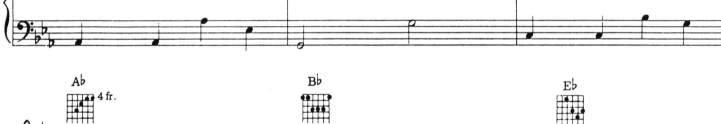

I WILL FOLLOW HIM
(I Will Follow You)

English Words by NORMAN GIMBEL and ARTHUR ALTMAN
French Words by JACQUES PLANTE
Music by J.W. STOLE and DEL ROMA

I WILL WAIT FOR YOU

from THE UMBRELLAS OF CHERBOURG

Music by MICHEL LEGRAND
Original French Text by JACQUES DEMY
English Words by NORMAN GIMBEL

IT GOES LIKE IT GOES

from the 20th Century Fox Film NORMA RAE

Words by NORMAN GIMBEL
Music by DAVID SHIRE

Expressively, but not too slowly

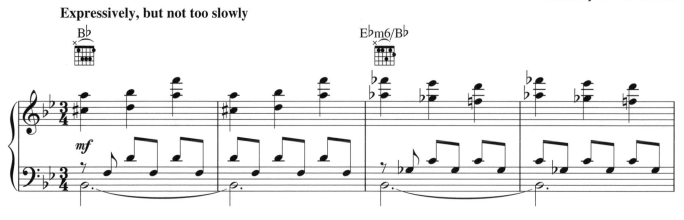

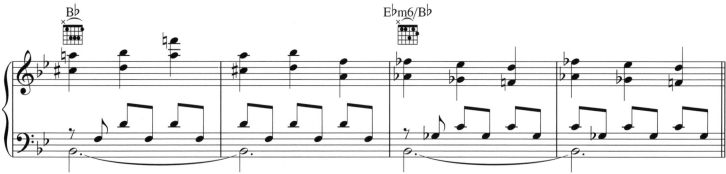

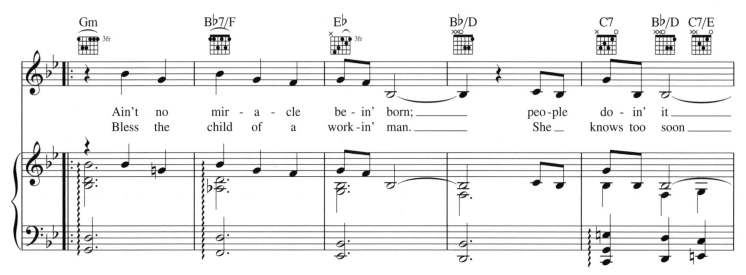

Ain't no mir-a-cle be-in' born;___ peo-ple do-in' it ___
Bless the child of a work-in' man. ___ She ___ knows too soon ___

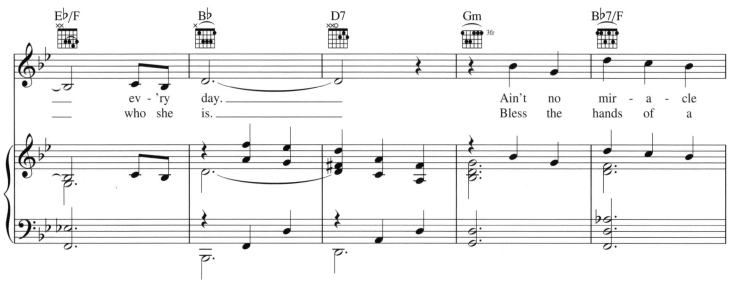

___ ev-'ry day. _____ Ain't no mir-a-cle
___ who she is. _____ Bless the hands of a

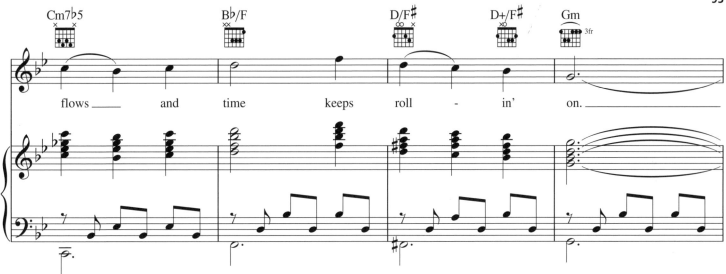

flows ___ and time keeps roll - in' on. ___

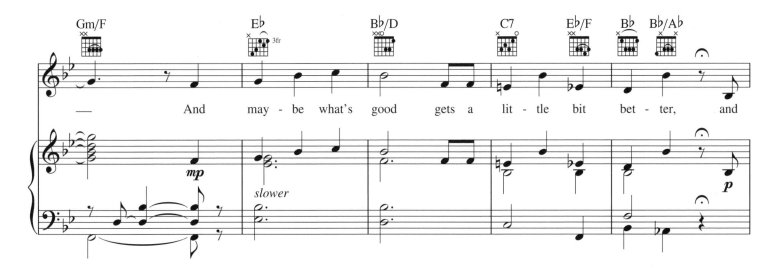

___ And may - be what's good gets a lit - tle bit bet - ter, and

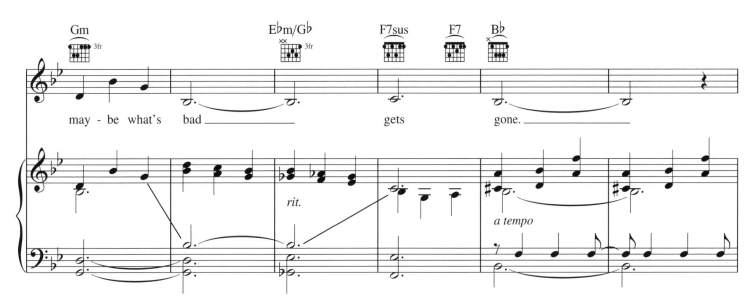

may - be what's bad ___ gets gone. ___

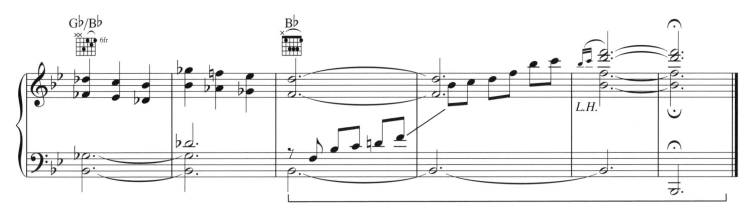

IT WAS ME
(C'était Moi)

English Words by NORMAN GIMBEL
French Words by MAURICE VIDALIN
Music by GILBERT BECAUD

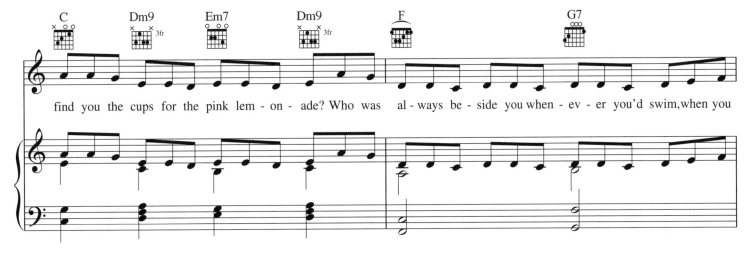

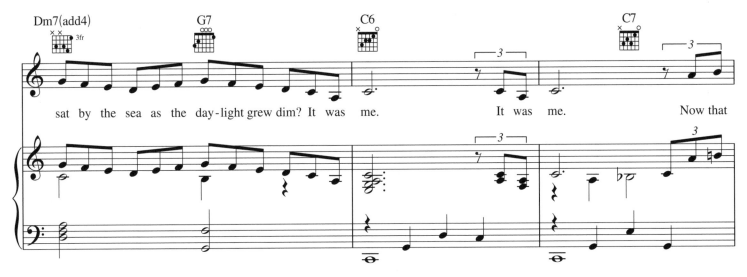

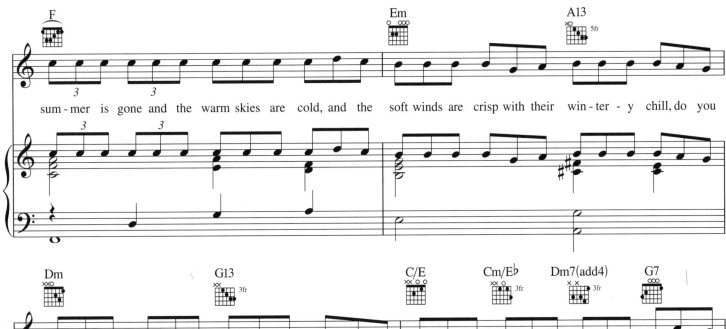

KILLING ME SOFTLY
WITH HIS SONG

Words by NORMAN GIMBEL
Music by CHARLES FOX

Smoothly, with a beat

life with his words, kill - ing me soft - ly _____

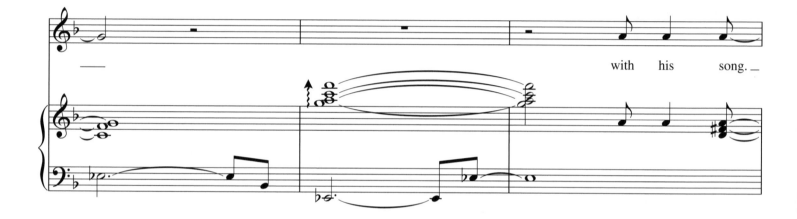

_____ with his song. _____

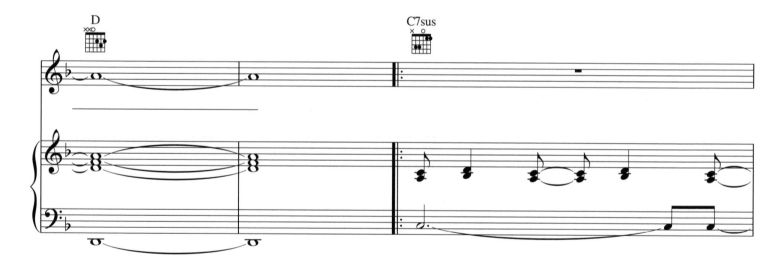

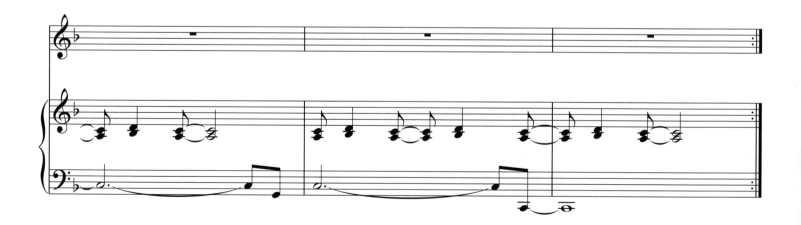

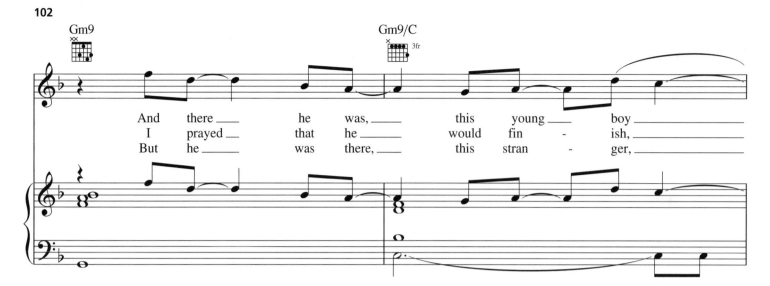

And there ___ he was, ___ this young ___ boy ___
I prayed ___ that he ___ this would fin - ish, ___
But he ___ was there, ___ this stran - ger, ___

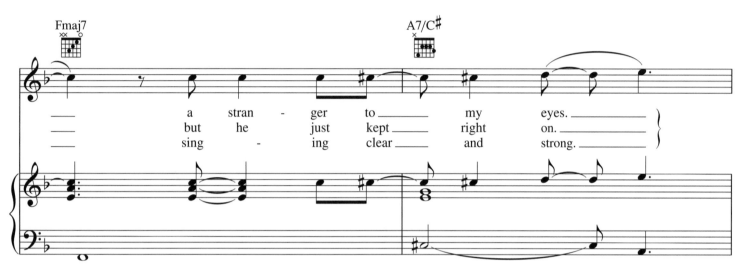

___ a stran - ger to ___ my eyes. ___
___ but he just kept ___ right on. ___
___ sing - ing clear ___ and strong. ___

Strum - ming my pain ___ with his fin - gers, ___

sing - ing my life ___ with his words. ___

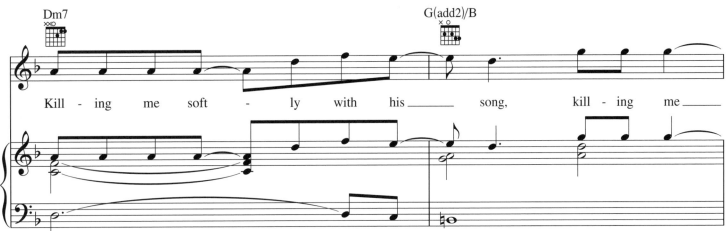

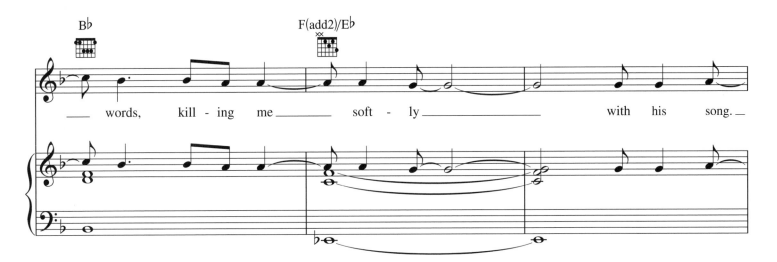

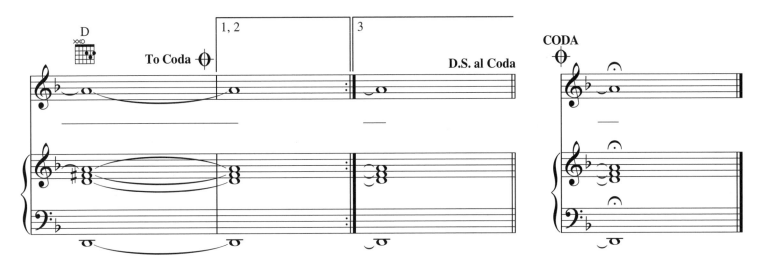

LIVE FOR LIFE
from LIVE FOR LIFE

Music by FRANCIS LAI
Words by NORMAN GIMBEL

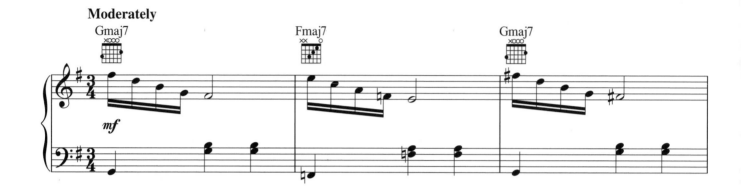

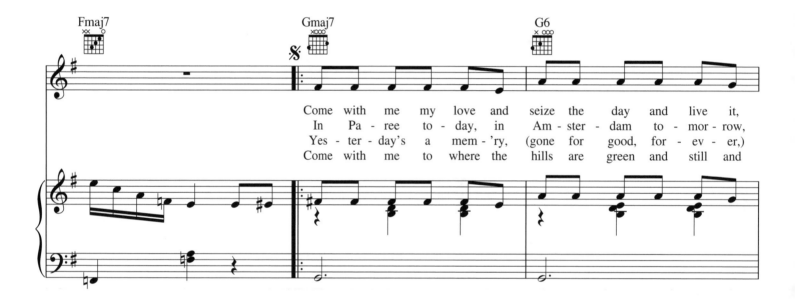

Come with me my love and seize the day and live it,
In Pa - ree to - day, in Am - ster - dam to - mor - row,
Yes - ter - day's a mem - 'ry, (gone for good, for - ev - er,)
Come with me to where the hills are green and still and

live it ful - ly, live it fast.
six - ty min - utes through the skies.
while to - mor - row is a guess.
filled with flow - ers to a - dore.

Nev - er think - ing once a -
Fly with me to see the
What is real is what is
Come with me to where the

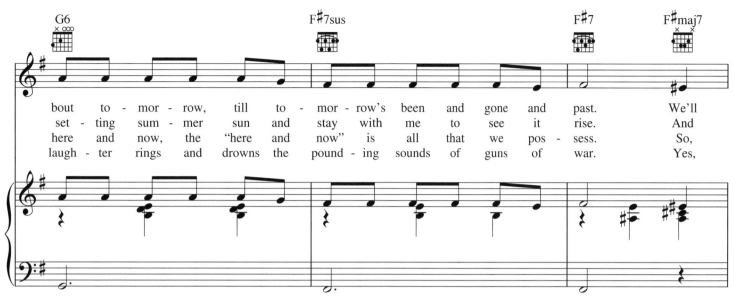

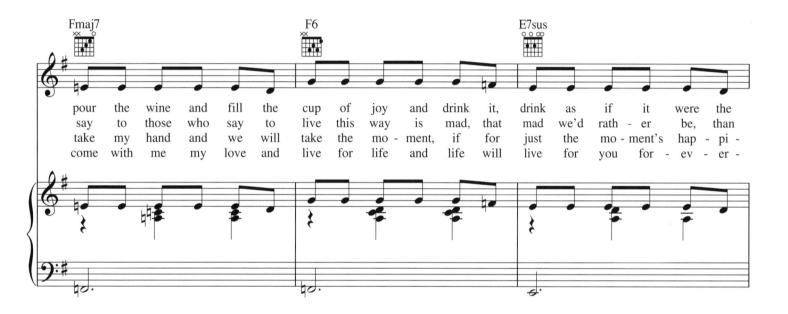

To Coda ⊕

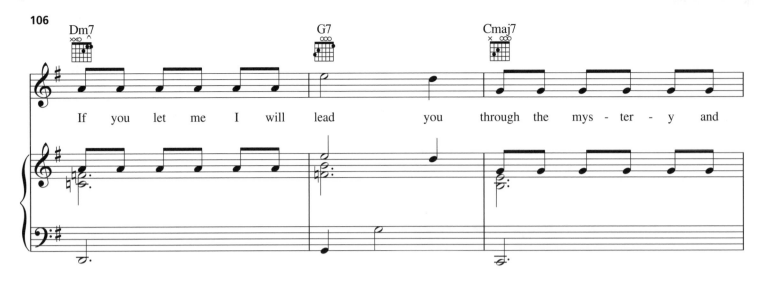

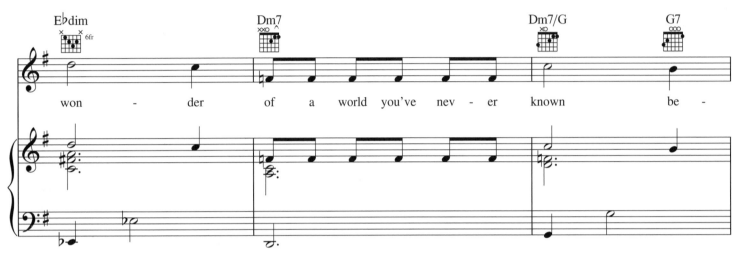

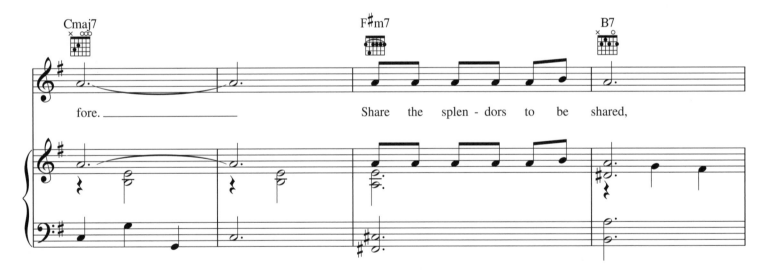

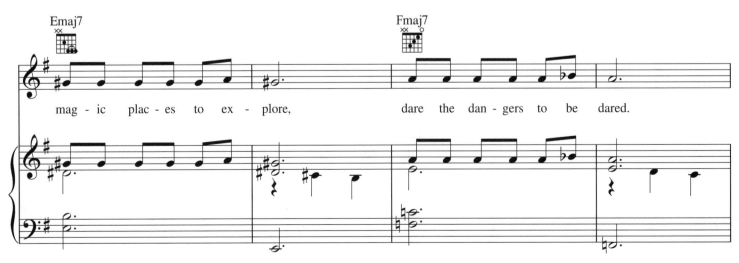

D.S. al Coda
(take repeat)

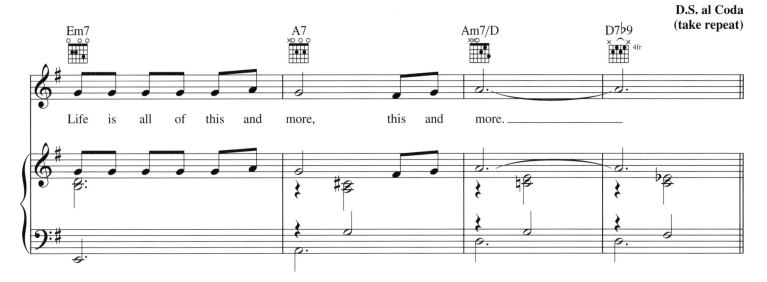

Life is all of this and more, this and more._____

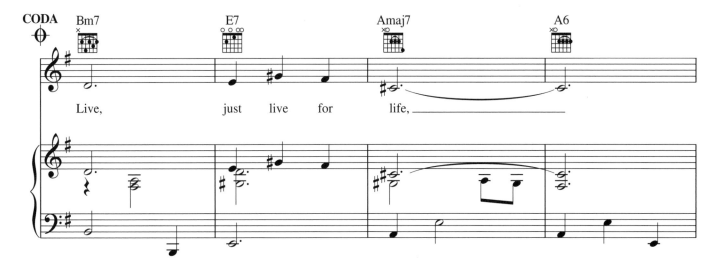

CODA

Live, just live for life,_____

Live, just live for life._____

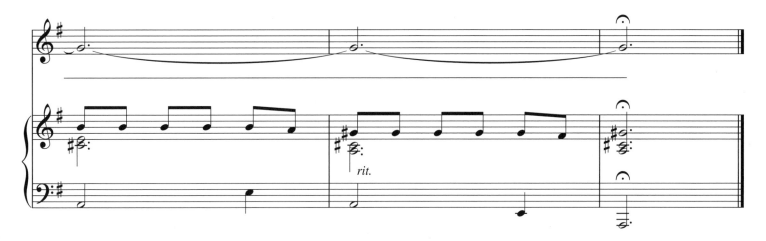

rit.

LOVE AMONG THE YOUNG

Words by NORMAN GIMBEL
Music by ALEC WILDER

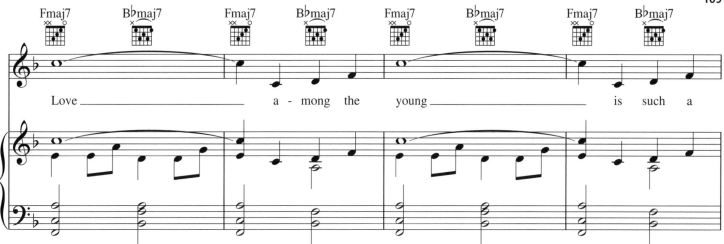

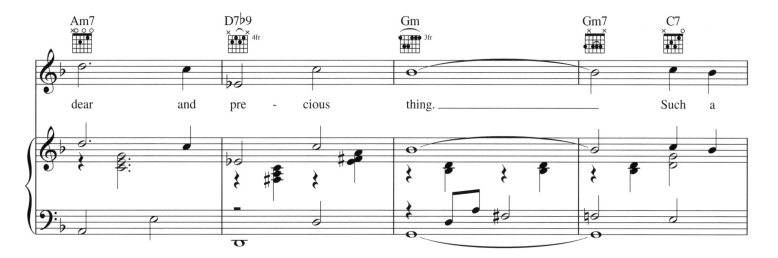

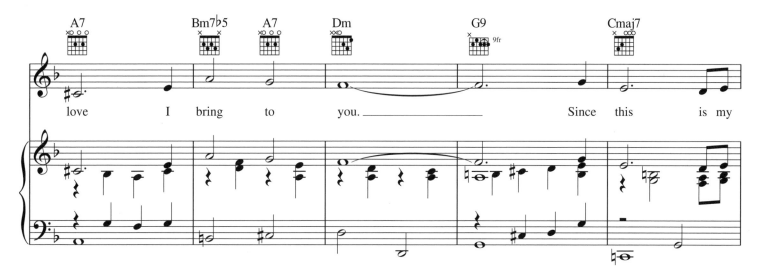

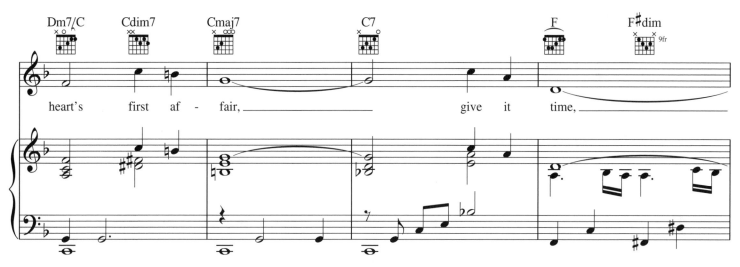

110

MAKING OUR DREAMS COME TRUE

Theme from the Paramount Television Series LAVERNE AND SHIRLEY

Words by NORMAN GIMBEL
Music by CHARLES FOX

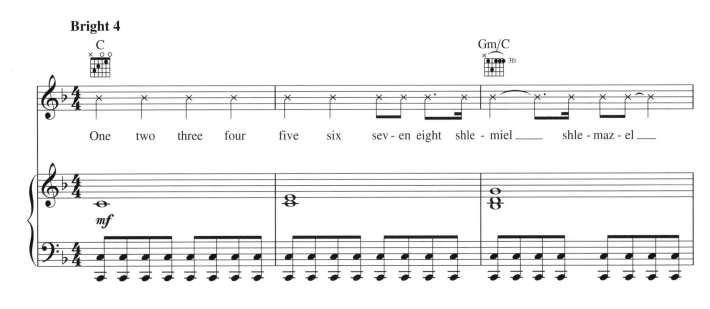

We're gon-na make ___ our dreams ___ come true,

do - in' it our ___ way. Noth - ing's gon - na turn ___ us back ___ now,

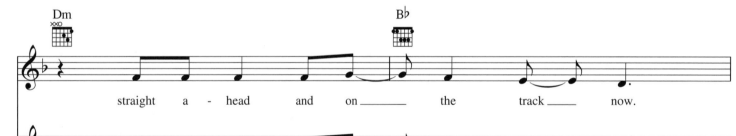

straight a - head and on ___ the track ___ now.

We're gon - na make ___ our dreams ___ come true,

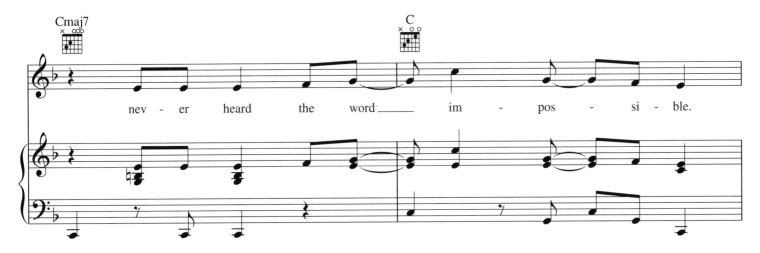

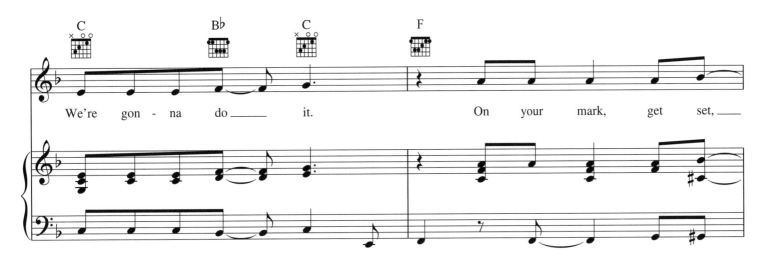

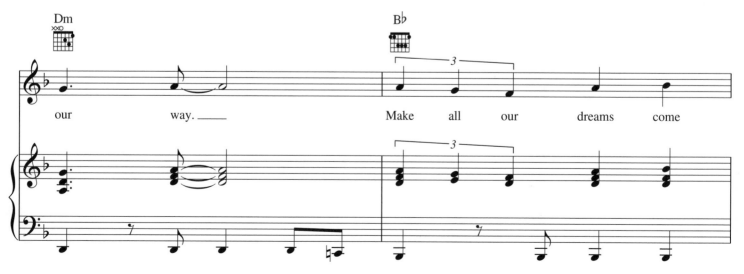

true, and do it our way, ___ yes our way. ___

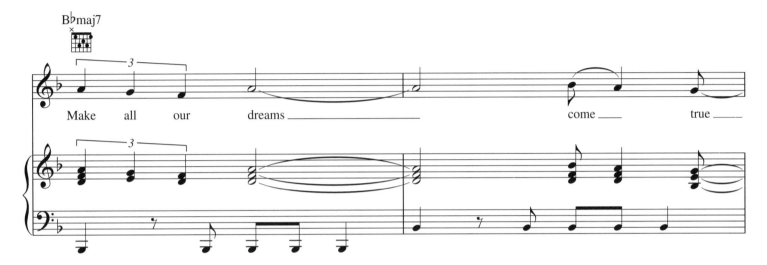

Make all our dreams _____ come ___ true ___

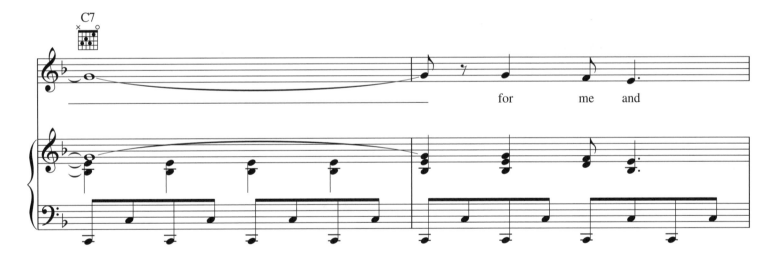

_____ for me and

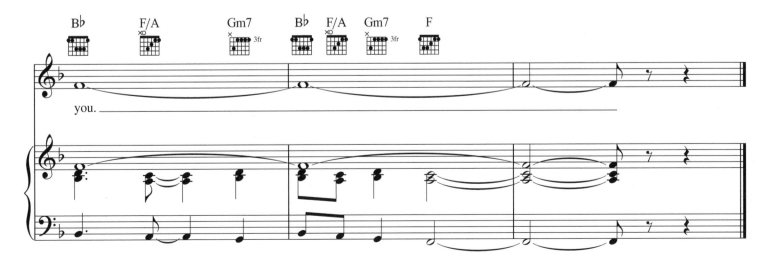

you. _____

A MAN AIN'T SUPPOSED TO CRY

Words and Music by NORMAN GIMBEL
and IRVING REID

MEDITATION
(Meditacáo)

Music by ANTONIO CARLOS JOBIM
Original Words by NEWTON MENDONCA
English Words by NORMAN GIMBEL

Lyrics:

In _____ my lone-li-ness _____ When you're gone _____
Though _____ you're far a-way _____ I have on-

___ and I'm all ___ by my-self ___ and I ___ need your ___ ca-ress. ___
-ly to close ___ my eyes ___ and you ___ are back ___ to stay. ___

I _____ just think ___ of you ___
I _____ just close ___ my eyes ___

MOONDUST

from the Paramount Film MEATBALLS

Words by NORMAN GIMBEL
Music by ELMER BERNSTEIN

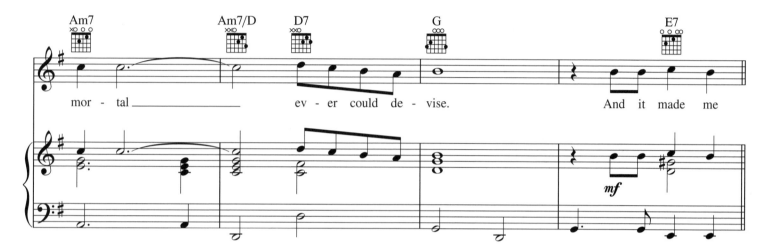

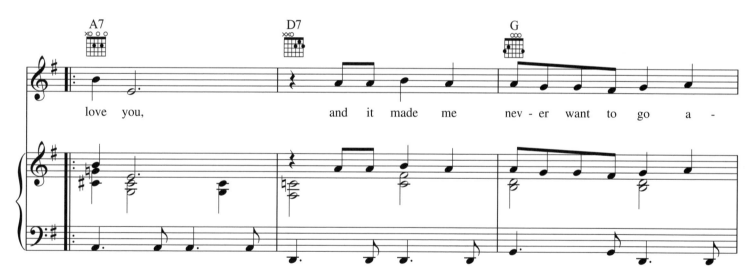

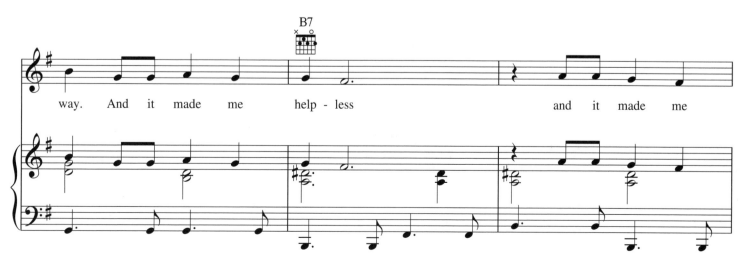

PAST THE AGE OF INNOCENCE

from the Broadway Musical THE CONQUERING HERO

Words by NORMAN GIMBEL
Music by MORRIS CHARLAP

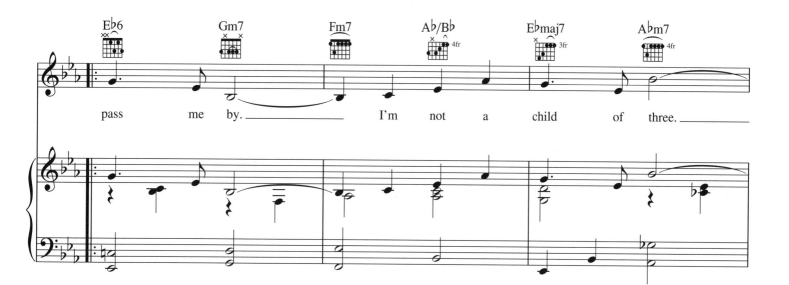

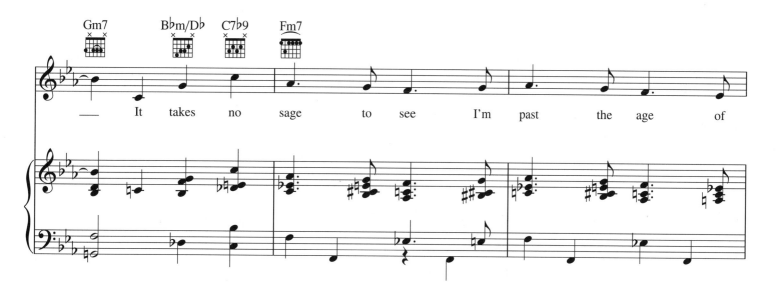

ONLY LOVE
(L'Amour en Héritage)
from MISTRAL'S DAUGHTER

English Words by NORMAN GIMBEL
French Words by PIERRE DELANO
Music by VLADIMIR COSMA

Slowly

On - ly love   can make a mem - o - ry.
J'ai re - çu   l'a - mour en hé - ri - tage

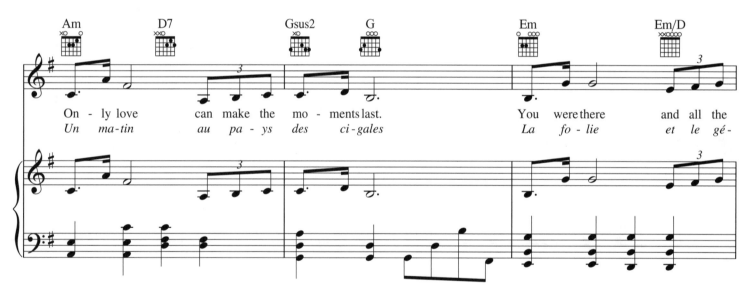

On - ly love   can make the mo - ments last.   You were there   and all the
Un ma - tin   au pa - ys des ci - gales   La fo - lie   et le gé -

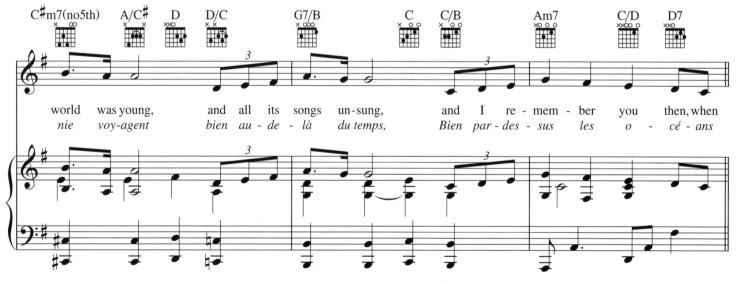

world was young,   and all its songs un - sung,   and I re - mem - ber you then, when
nie voy - agent   bien au - de - là du temps,   Bien par - des - sus les o - cé - ans

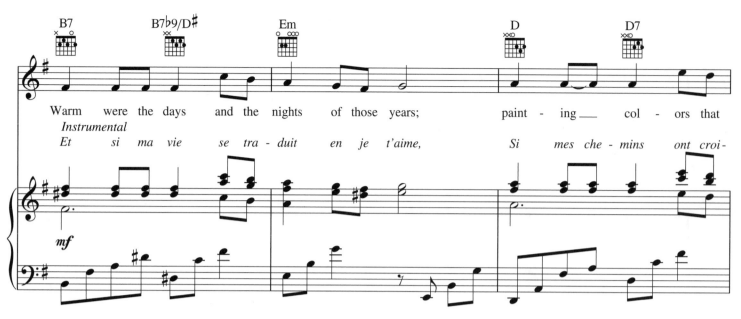

Warm were the days and the nights of those years; paint - ing___ col - ors that
Instrumental
Et si ma vie se tra - duit en je t'aime, Si mes che - mins ont croi-

out - shined the sun. All of the words and the dreams and the tears live in
sé des tor - rents, On est tou - jours un oi - seau de bo - hème une en-

my re - mem - brance. } On - ly love can make a mem - o - ry.
End instrumental }
fant du prin - temps J'ai re - çu l'a-mour en hé - ri - tage

rit. *a tempo*

PINE TOP'S BOOGIE

Words by NORMAN GIMBEL
Music by CLARENCE "PINE TOP" SMITH

Not too fast

There's a fel - la___ plays pi - an - o___ made of pine wood,___ real - ly

fine wood,___ you should know him,___ folks who know him___ call him Pine Top,___

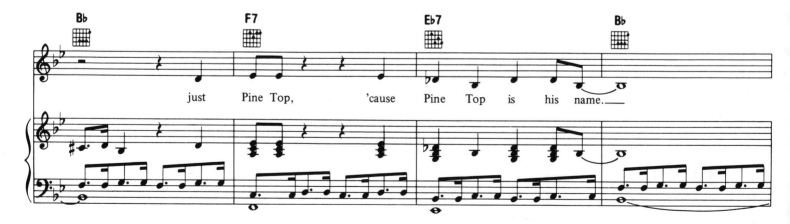

just Pine Top, 'cause Pine Top is his name.___

He plays a trick-y boog-ie beat that makes you want to stomp your feet. The show be -

gins at nine o-clock and then the room be-gins to rock, he's got a mel-low kind of style and you can

spot it from a mile, he plays pi-an-o in a groove that says, "get up, go on and move." So dress in

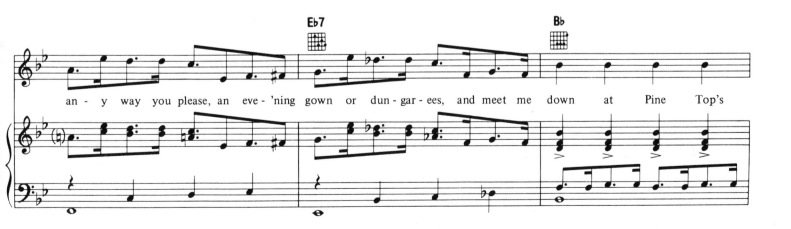

an-y way you please, an eve-'ning gown or dun-gar-ees, and meet me down at Pine Top's

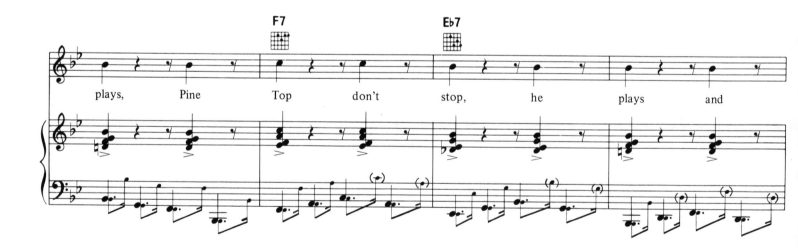

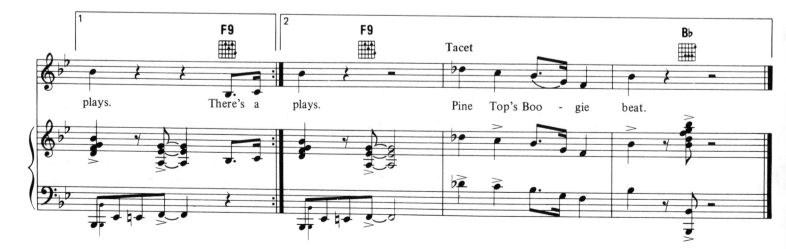

READY TO TAKE A CHANCE AGAIN
(Love Theme)
from the Paramount Picture FOUL PLAY

Words by NORMAN GIMBEL
Music by CHARLES FOX

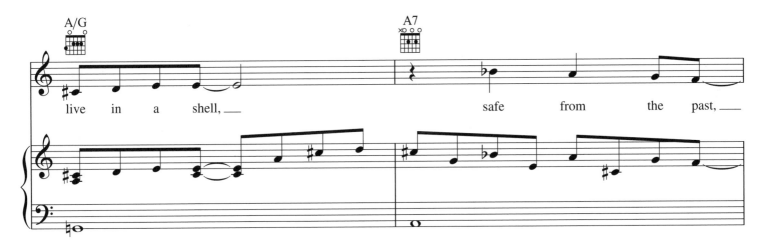

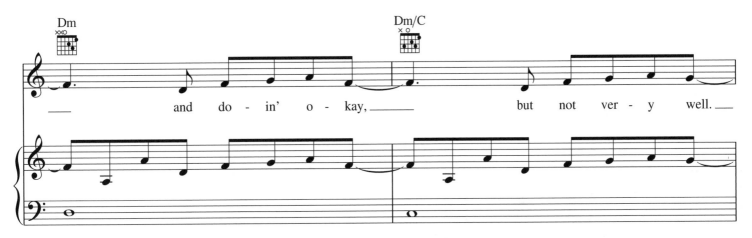

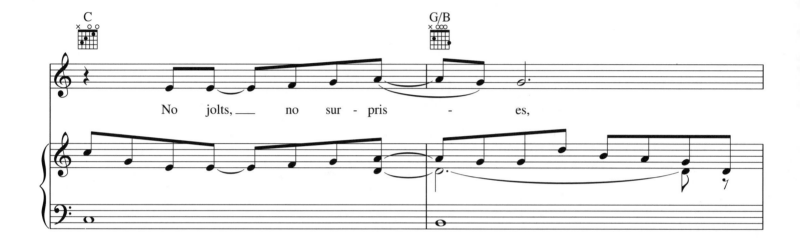

No jolts, ___ no sur - pris - es,

no cri - sis a - ris - es. My life ___ goes a - long ___

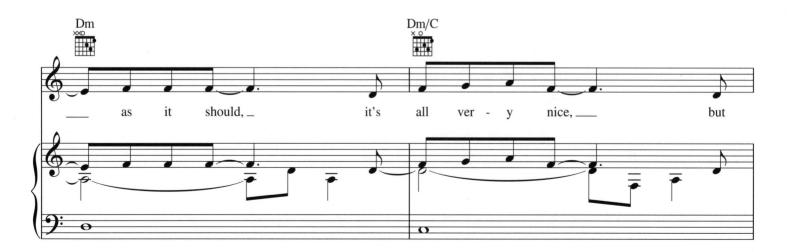

___ as it should, _ it's all ver - y nice, ___ but

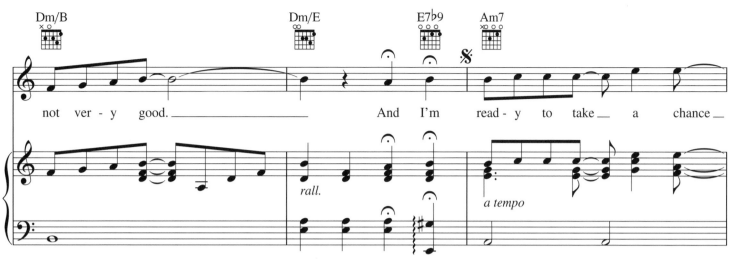

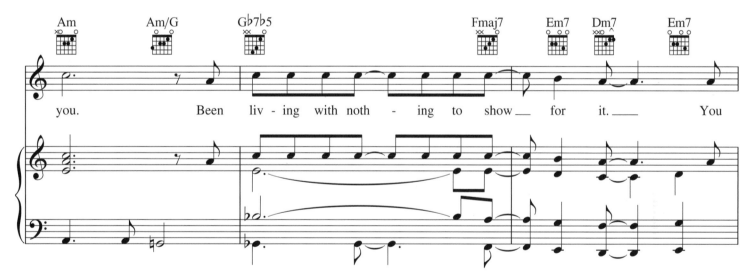

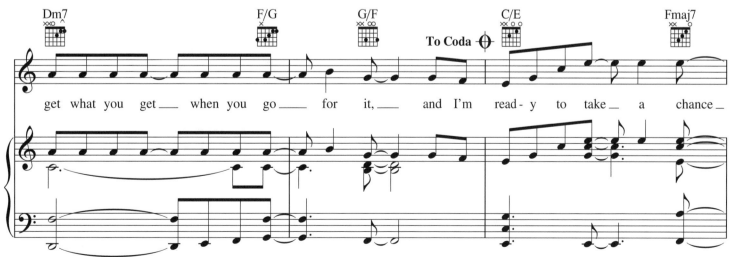

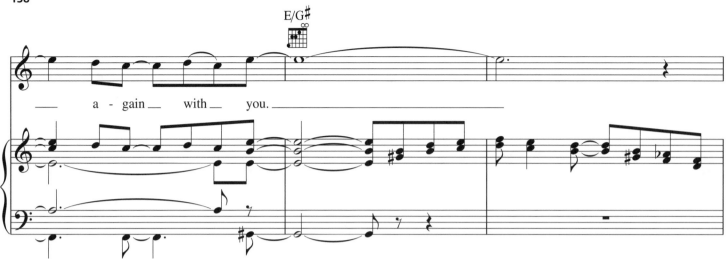

a - gain with you.

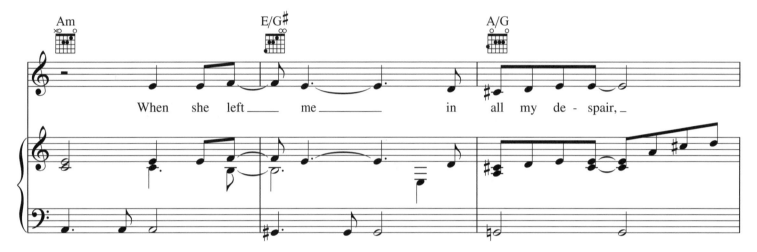

When she left me in all my de - spair,

I just held on. My hopes were all gone, then

D.S. al Coda

I found you there. And I'm

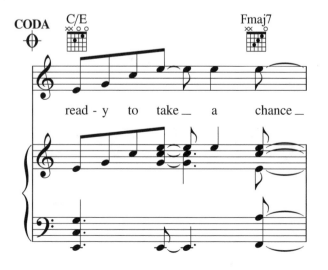

ready to take a chance

139

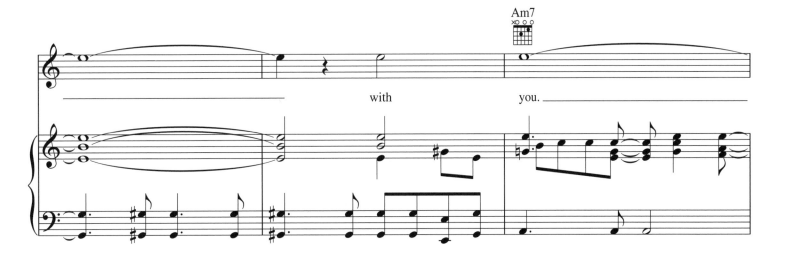

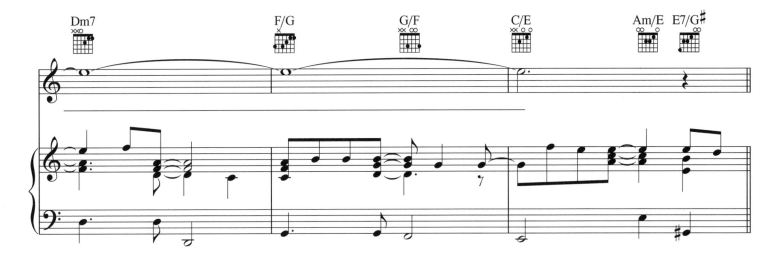

Repeat ad lib. and Fade

RICOCHET ROMANCE

Words and Music by NORMAN GIMBEL,
LARRY COLEMAN and JOE DARION

Brightly

They

warned me when you kissed me _____ your love would
knew the the day I met you, _____ you love had a
(you)
(we) an- nounced our wed - ding _____ you made me

ric- o- chet. _____ Your lips would find an-
rov- in' eye. _____ I thought that I could
might- y proud. _____ I whis- pered two was

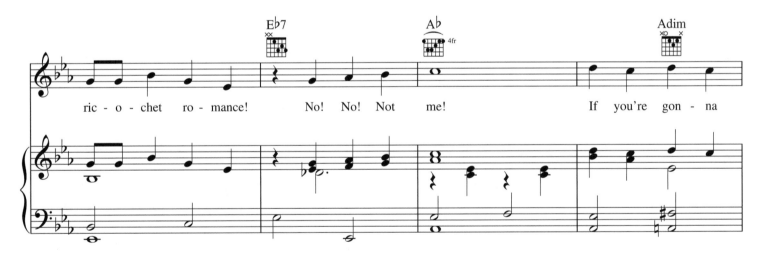

SO NICE
(Summer Samba)

Original Words and Music by MARCOS VALLE
and PAULO SERGIO VALLE
English Words by NORMAN GIMBEL

Relaxed Bossa Nova

145

SLOW HOT WIND
(Lujon)

Words by NORMAN GIMBEL
Music by HENRY MANCINI

SONG OF THE SABIÁ
(Sabiá)

English Words by NORMAN GIMBEL
Music by ANTONIO CARLOS JOBIM
Original Portuguese Lyric by CHICO BUARQUE DE HOLLANDA

149

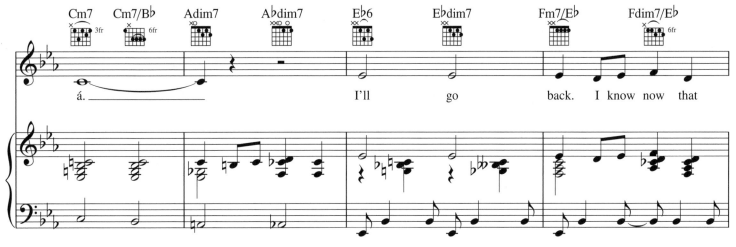

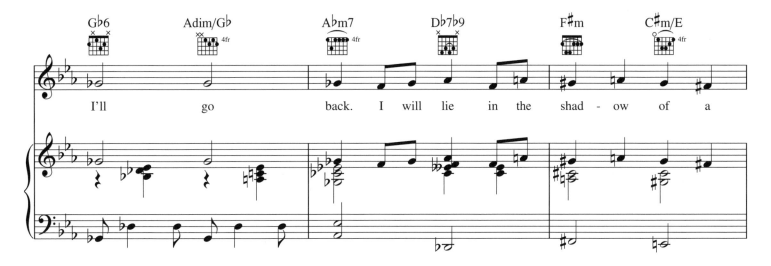

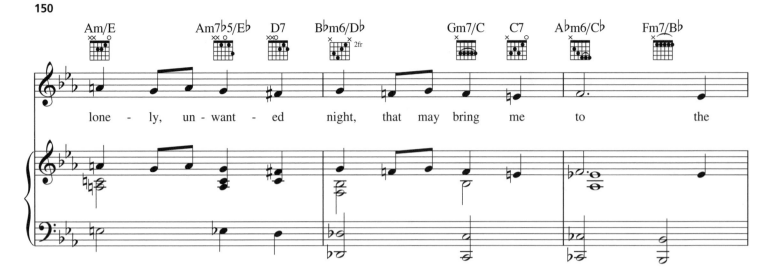

lone - ly, un - want - ed night, that may bring me to the

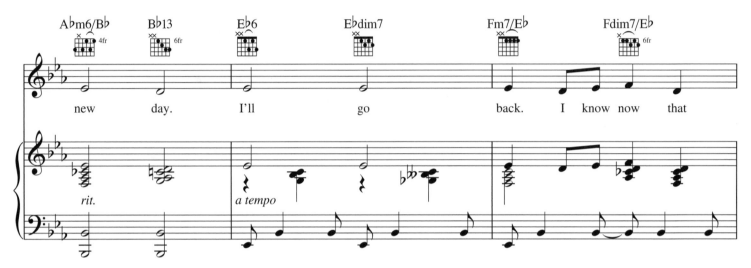

new day. I'll go back. I know now that

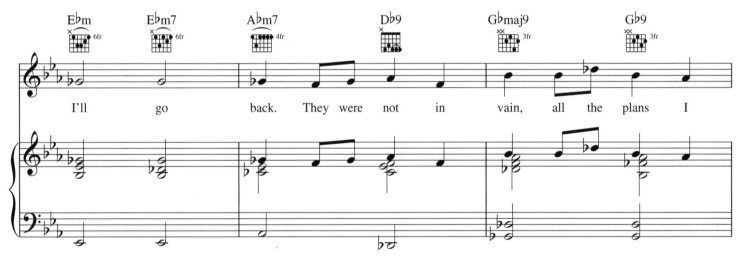

I'll go back. They were not in vain, all the plans I

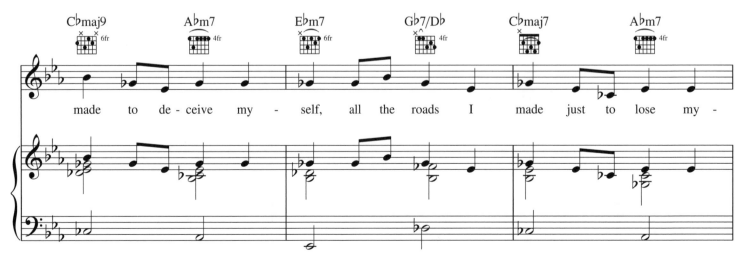

made to de - ceive my - self, all the roads I made just to lose my -

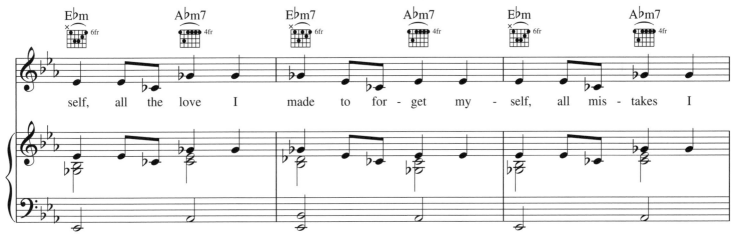

self, all the love I made to for- get my - self, all mis- takes I

D.S. al Coda

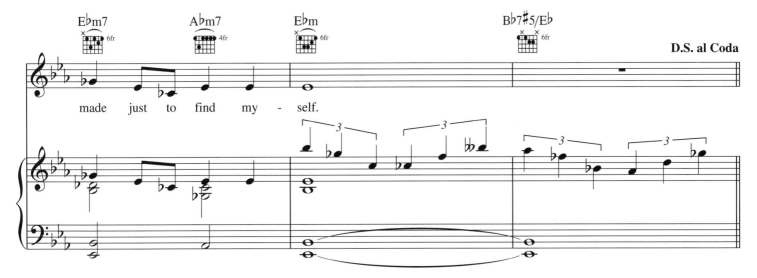

made just to find my - self.

CODA

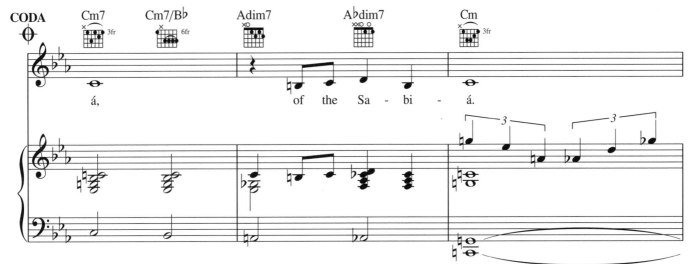

á, of the Sa- bi - á.

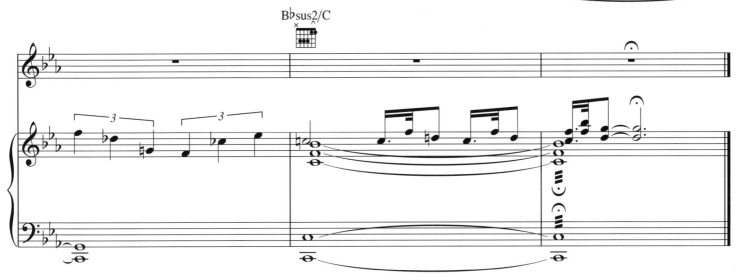

TIME FOR ME TO GO

Words by NORMAN GIMBEL
Music by CHARLES FOX

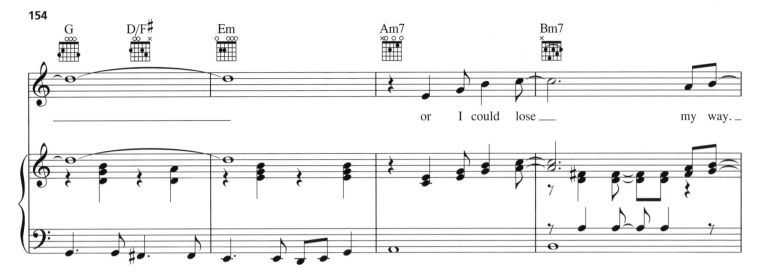

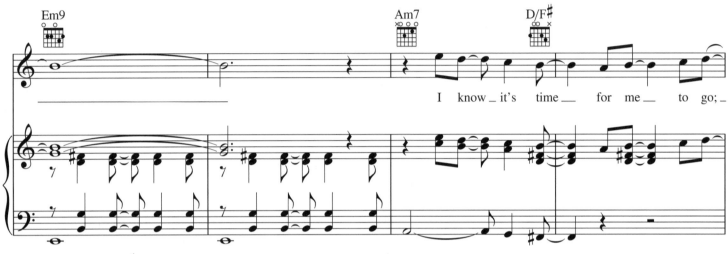

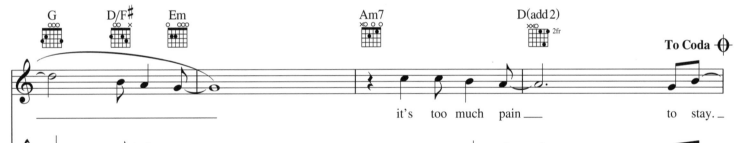

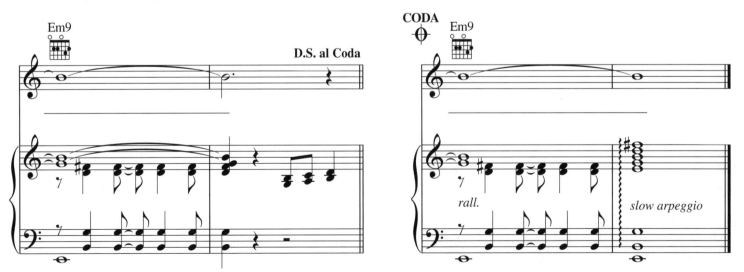

SWAY
(Quien Será)

English Words by NORMAN GIMBEL
Spanish Words and Music by PABLO BELTRAN RUIZ

When ma-rim-ba rhy-thms start to play, dance with me,
Quien se-rá la que me quie-ra a mi Quien se-rá

make me sway.___ Like the la-zy o-cean hugs the shore,
Quien se-rá___ Quien se-rá la que me dé su a-mor

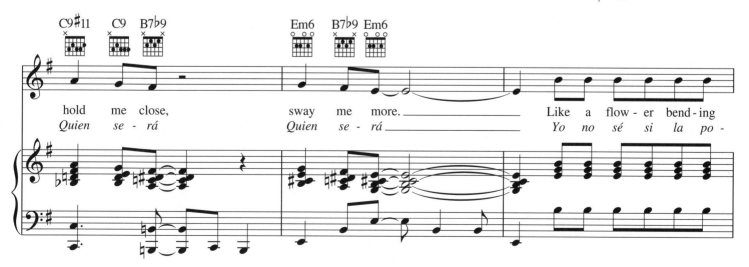

hold me close, sway me more._____ Like a flow-er bend-ing
Quien se-rá Quien se-rá_____ Yo no sé si la po-

SWEET HAPPY LIFE
(Samba de Orpheo)
Theme from BLACK ORPHEUS

English Words by NORMAN GIMBEL
Original Portuguese Words by ANTONIO MARIA
Music by LUIZ BONFA

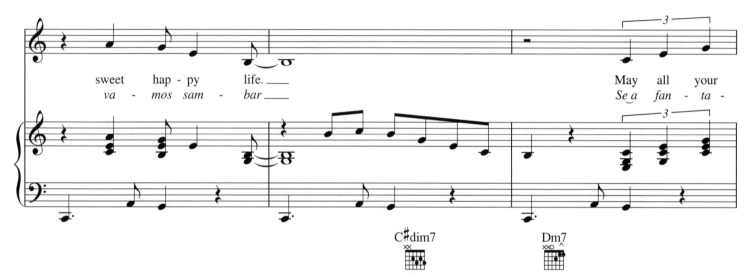

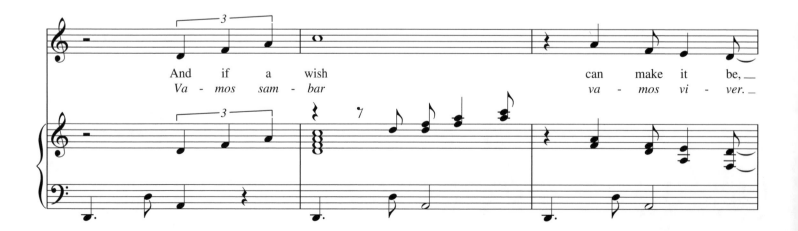

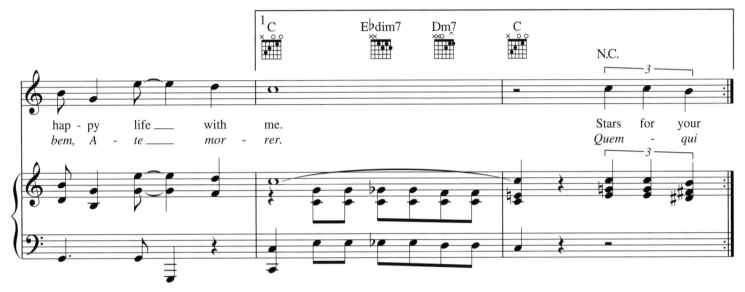

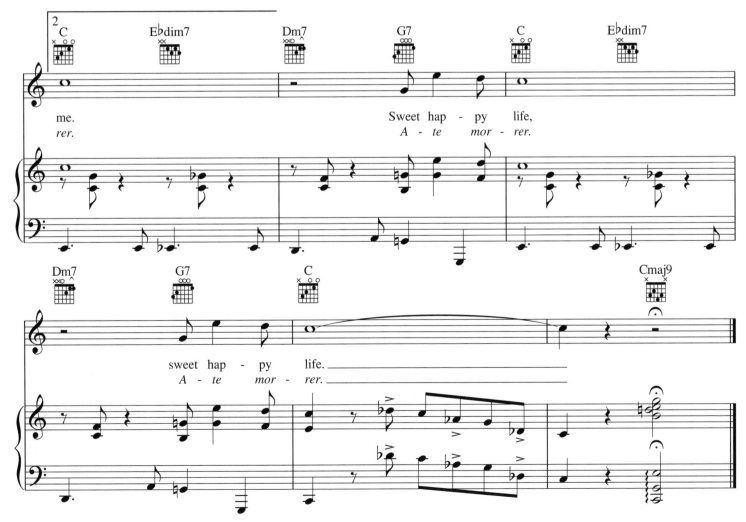

TIME

from the Film THE ONLY THRILL

Words by NORMAN GIMBEL
Music by PETER RODGERS MELNICK

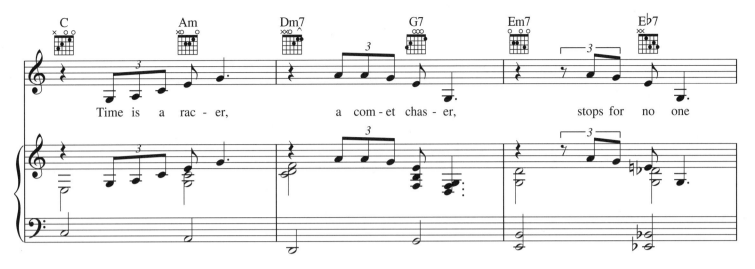

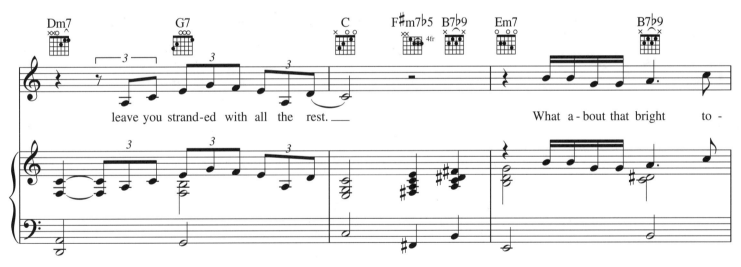

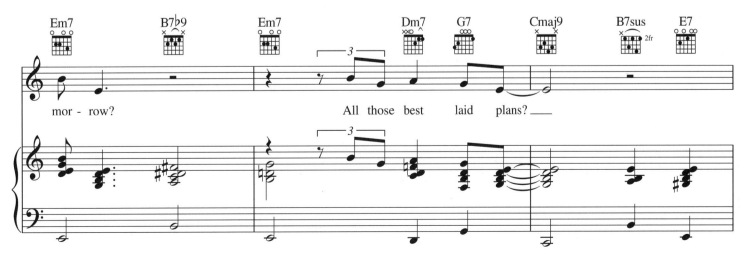

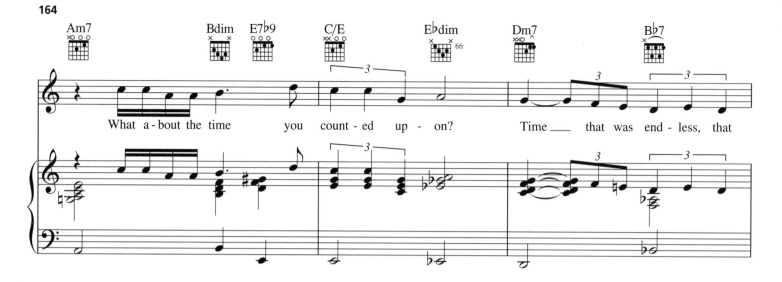

What a-bout the time you count-ed up-on? Time ___ that was end-less, that

now is gone? ___ Love nev-er tast-ed is love that's wast-ed,

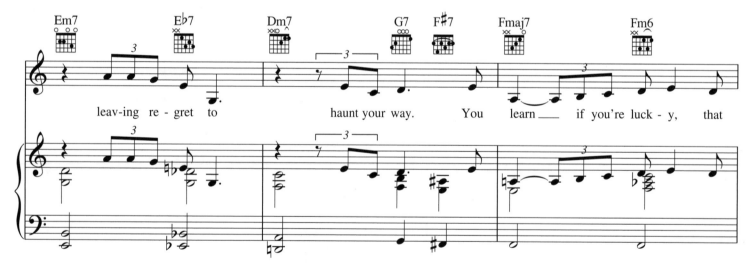

leav-ing re-gret to haunt your way. You learn ___ if you're luck-y, that

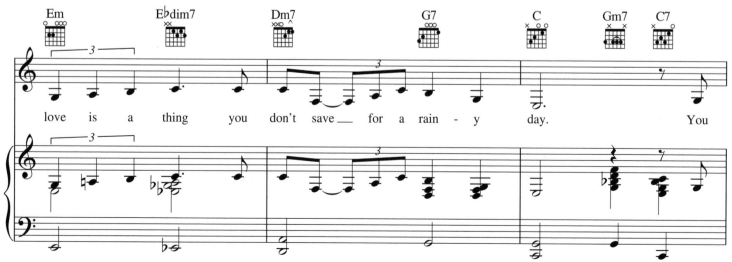

love is a thing you don't save ___ for a rain-y day. You

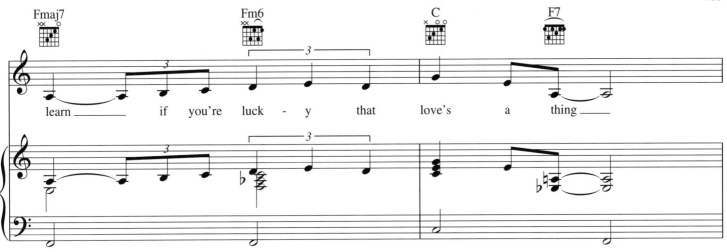

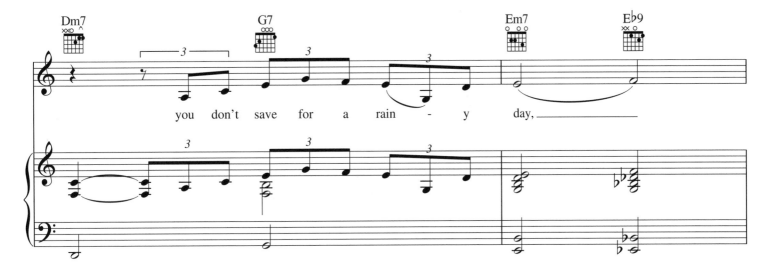

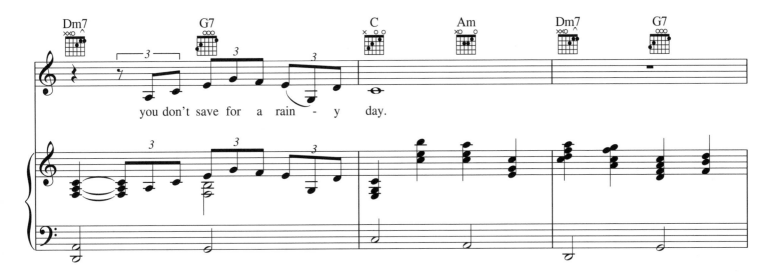

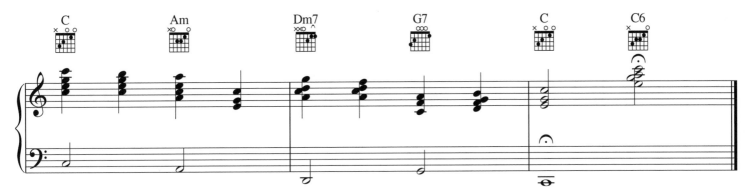

TIME IS A GIFT

from the MGM Film THE PHANTOM TOLLBOOTH

Words by NORMAN GIMBEL
Music by LEE POCKRISS

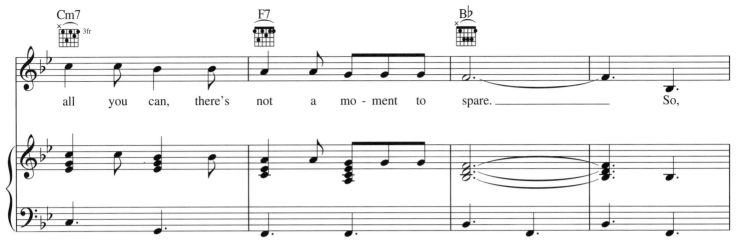

all you can, there's not a mo-ment to spare. _____ So,

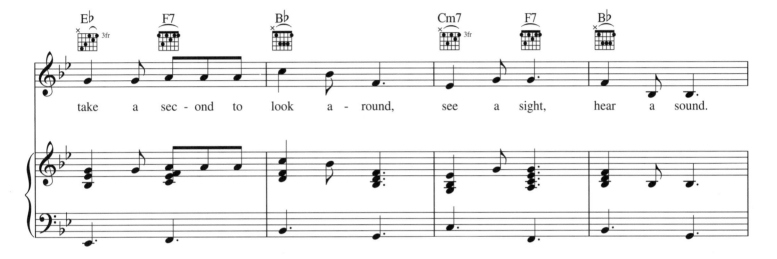

take a sec-ond to look a-round, see a sight, hear a sound.

Take a min-ute to con-cen-trate, an-a-lyze, _____

con-tem-plate. _____ Take an hour ___ and change the fate of the

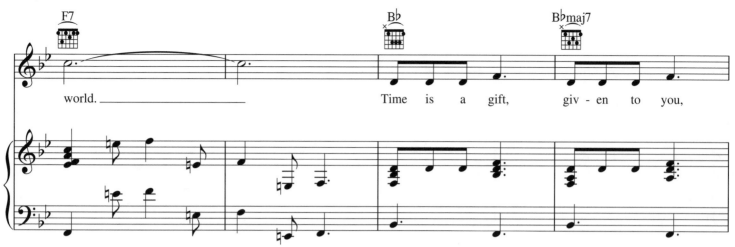

world. _____ Time is a gift, giv-en to you,

giv-en to give you the time you need, the time you need to have the time of your

life. _____ Time, ticks

has-ti-ly a-way. Take time to save it ev-'ry

day. Time saved in the nick of time

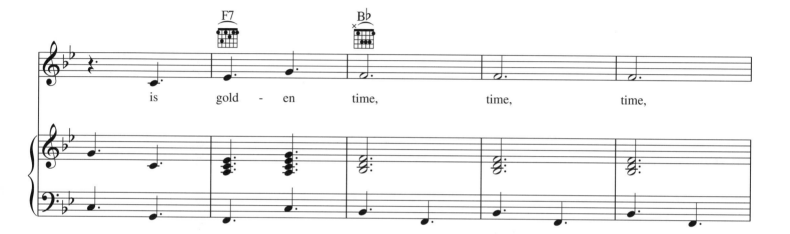

is gold - en time, time, time,

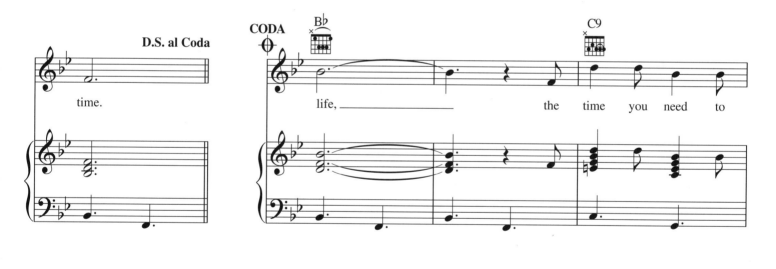

D.S. al Coda

time.

CODA

life, _____ the time you need to

have the time of your life. _____

TOGETHER

Words by NORMAN GIMBEL
Music by CHARLES FOX

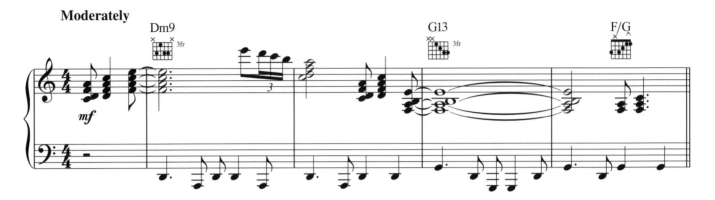

She/He clos-es her/his eyes ___ and she/he makes mu - sic. ___
I tell her/him my dreams _ and all my se - crets. ___

She/He clos-es her/his eyes ___ and I close mine. ___
I tell her/him my dreams _ and she/he tells hers. ___ / his. ___

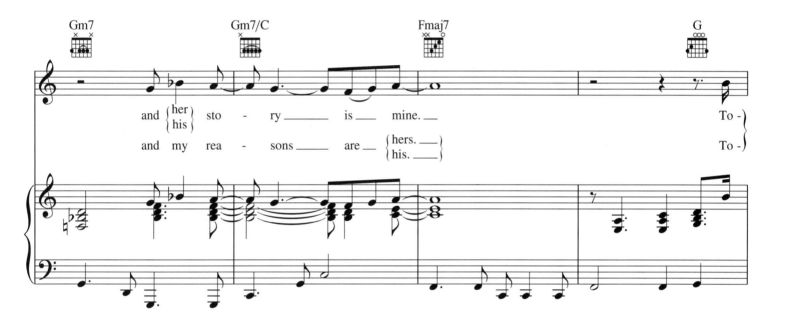

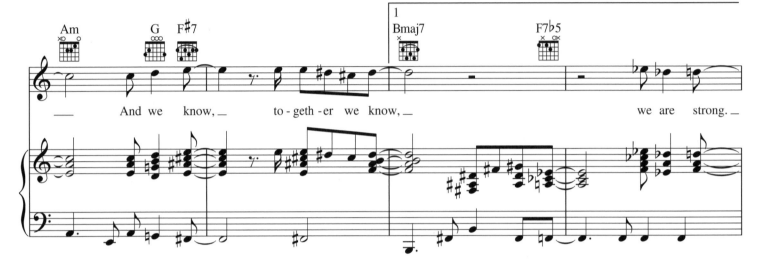

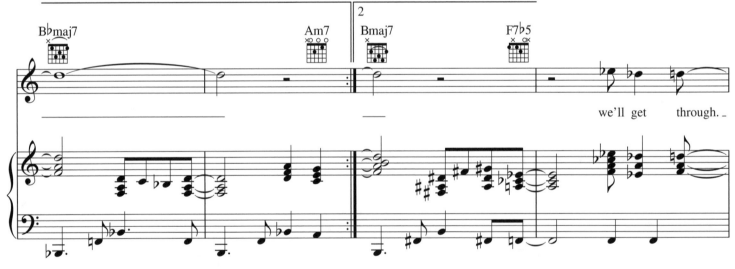

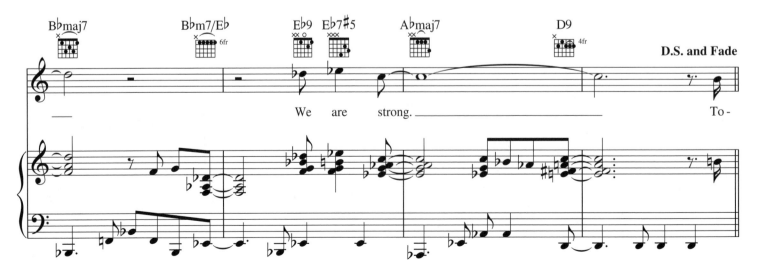

TRACES

Words by NORMAN GIMBEL
Music by NELLY RANSOM GIMBEL

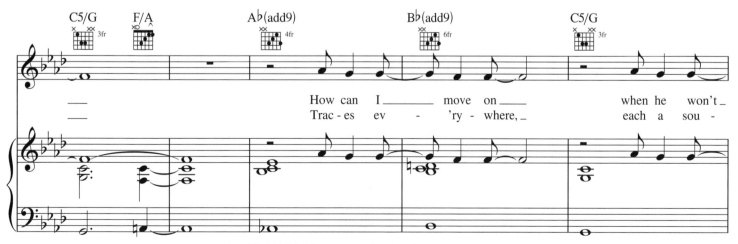

Lyrics (as they appear under the staves):

Some old pho - to - graph, ___
Mem -'ries that ___ should fade, ___

ech - oes of ___ his laugh, ___ trac - es of ___ him ev - 'ry - where. ___
but in - stead ___ pa - rade, ___ put - ting him ___ be - fore _ my eyes. ___

How can I ___ move on ___ when he won't
Trac - es ev - 'ry - where, ___ each a sou -

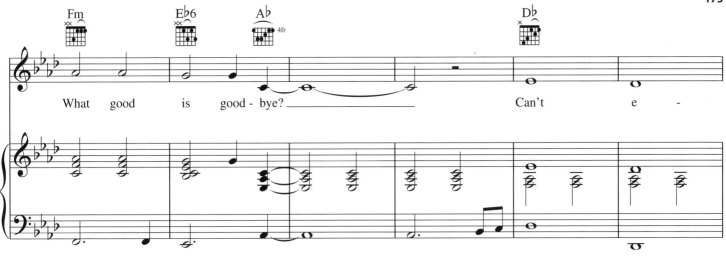

What good is good - bye? _____ Can't e -

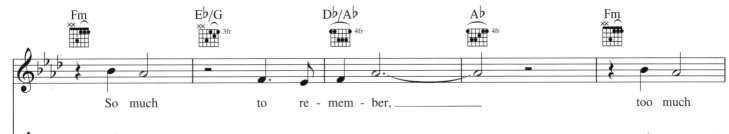

rase him. _____ Can't re - place him. _____

So much to re - mem - ber, _____ too much

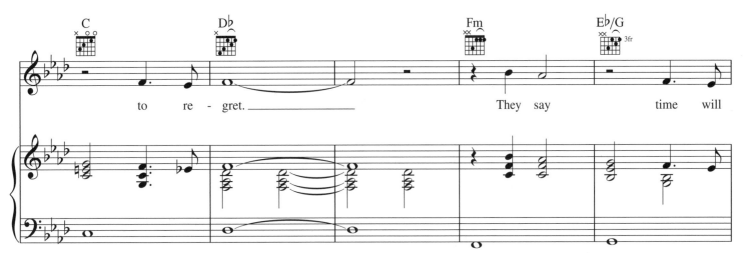

to re - gret. _____ They say time will

WATCH WHAT HAPPENS

from THE UMBRELLAS OF CHERBOURG

Music by MICHEL LEGRAND
Original French Text by JACQUES DEMY
English Lyrics by NORMAN GIMBEL

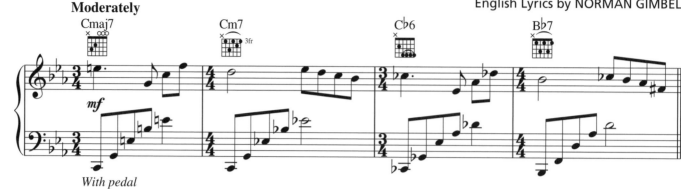

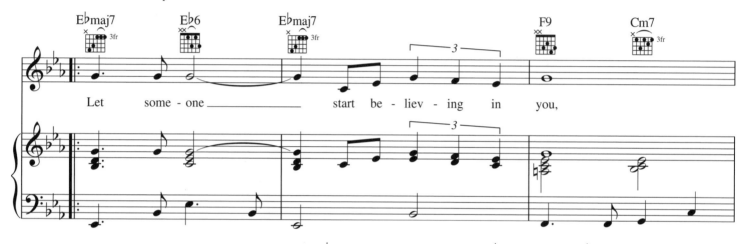

Let some-one _____ start be-liev-ing in you,

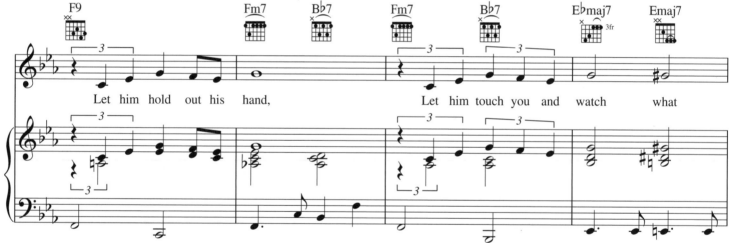

Let him hold out his hand, Let him touch you and watch what

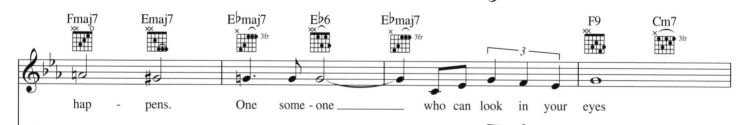

hap - pens. One some-one _____ who can look in your eyes

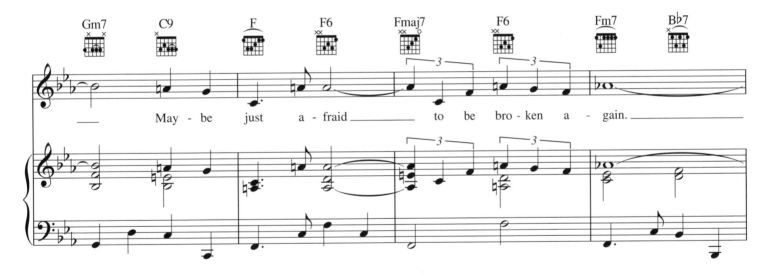

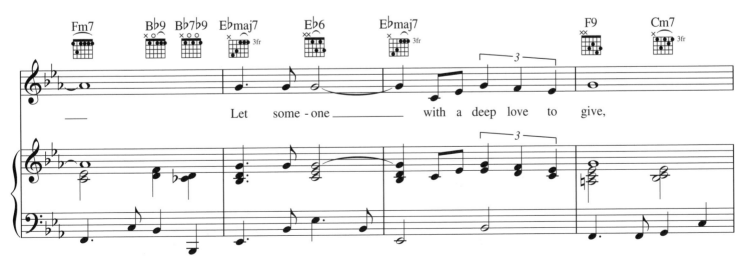

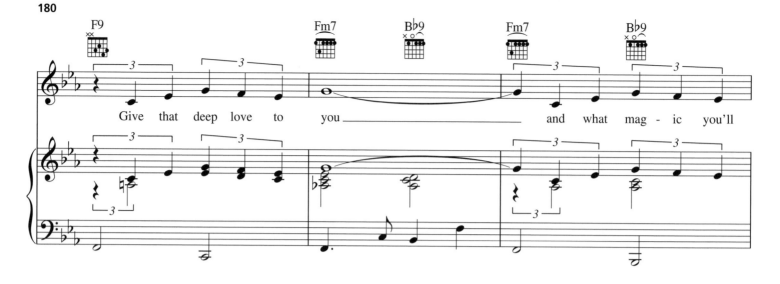

Give that deep love to you _____ and what mag - ic you'll

see: Let some - one give his heart, Some -

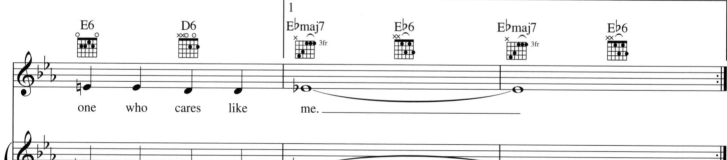

1

one who cares like me. _____

2

me. _____

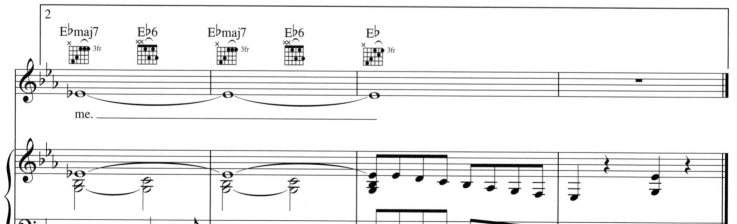

WE COULD HAVE IT ALL

from the Universal Film THE LAST MARRIED COUPLE IN AMERICA

Words by NORMAN GIMBEL
Music by CHARLES FOX

WELCOME TO MY WORLD

from the Warner Bros. Film A TROLL IN CENTRAL PARK

Words by NORMAN GIMBEL
Music by ROBERT FOLK

Do you see it through the trees, do you see a mag-ic place? Do you

feel a ting-ly breeze blow-ing friend-ly on your face?

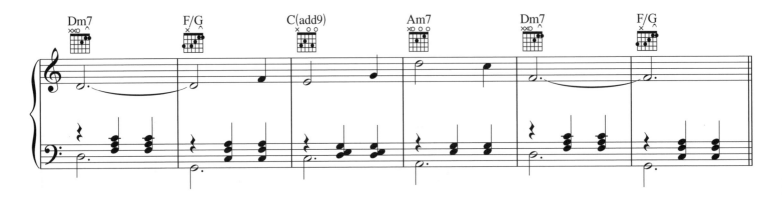

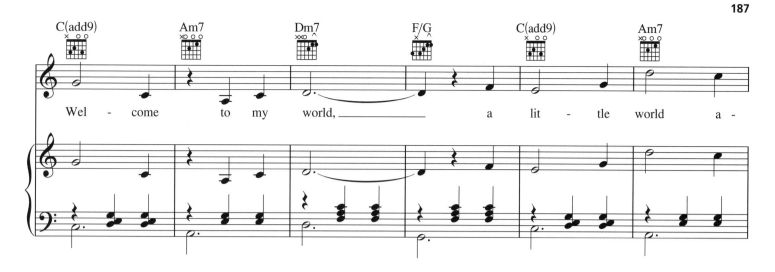

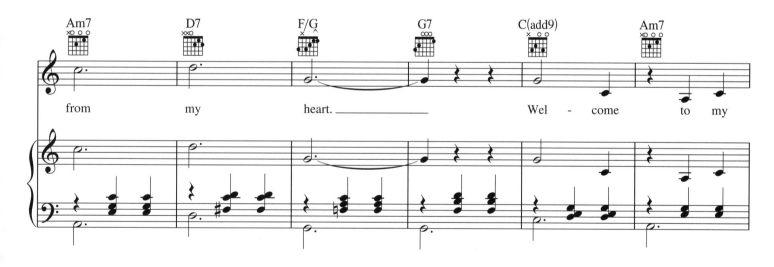

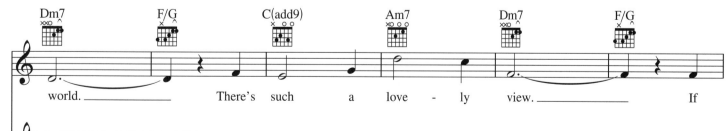

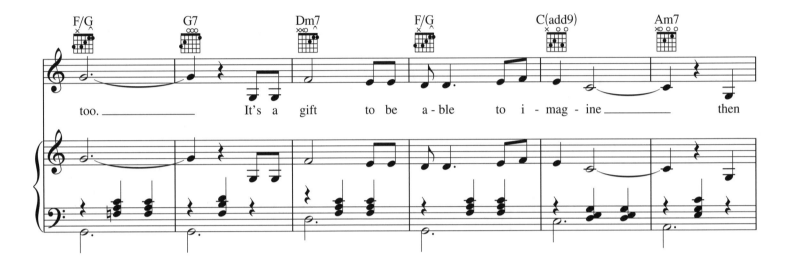

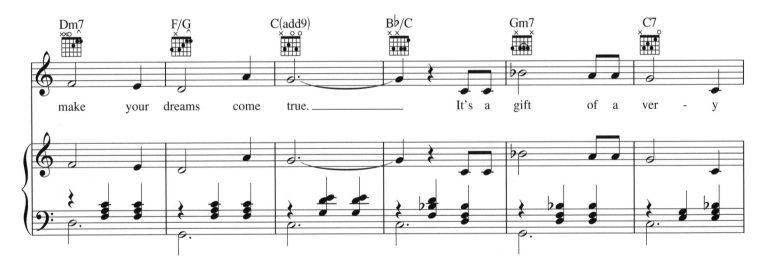

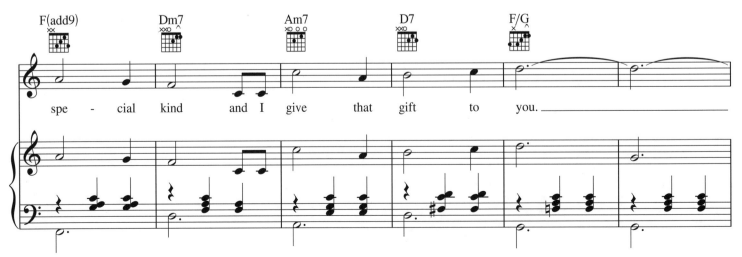

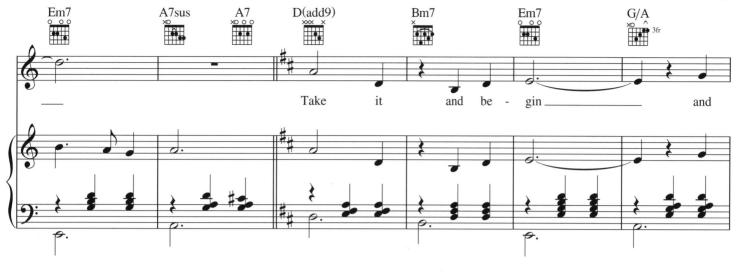

Take it and be - gin _____ and

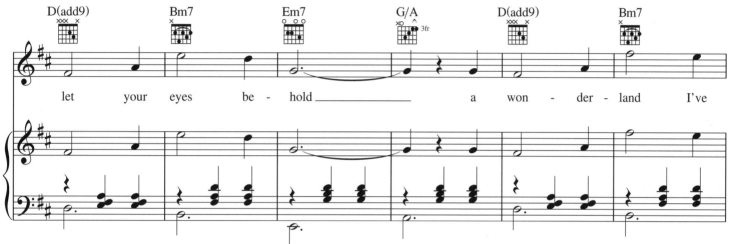

let your eyes be - hold _____ a won - der - land I've

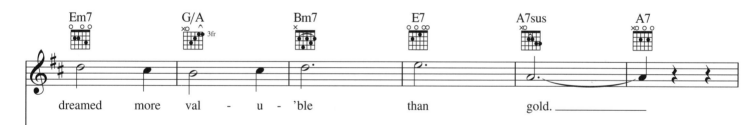

dreamed more val - u - 'ble than gold. _____

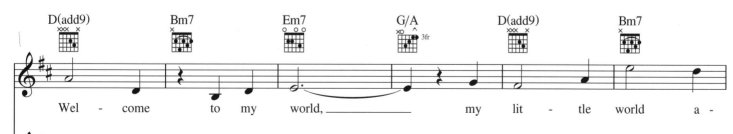

Wel - come to my world, _____ my lit - tle world a -

part, _____ a place my dreams have made with wish - es

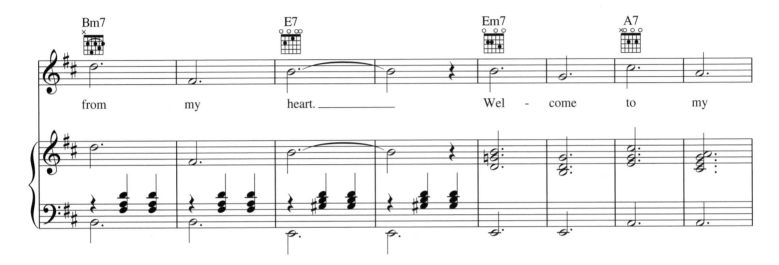

from my heart. _____ Wel - come to my

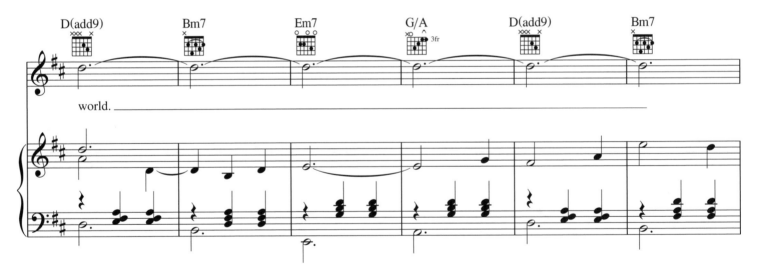

world. _____

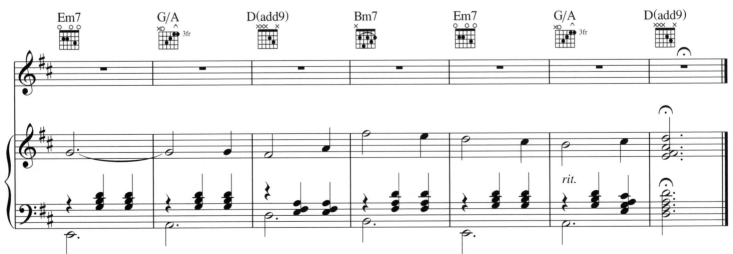

WHERE'S POPPA
from the United Artists Film WHERE'S POPPA?

Words by NORMAN GIMBEL
Music by JACK Z. ELLIOTT

A WHALE OF A TALE

from Walt Disney's 20,000 LEAGUES UNDER THE SEA

Words and Music by NORMAN GIMBEL
and AL HOFFMAN

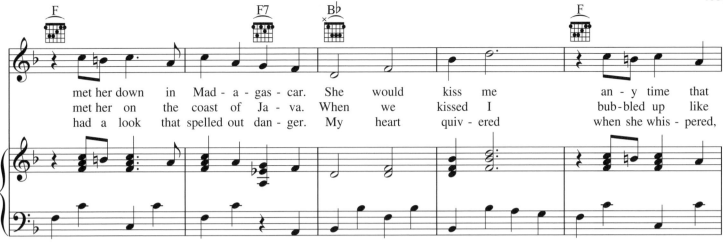

met her down in Mad - a - gas - car. She would kiss me an - y time that
met her on the coast of Ja - va. When we kissed I bub-bled up like
had a look that spelled out dan - ger. My heart quiv - ered when she whis - pered,

I would ask her. Then one eve - ning her flame of love blew out.
mol - ten la - va. Then she gave me the scare of my young life.
"Hi there, stran - ger!" Bought her trin - kets that sail - ors can't af - ford. And

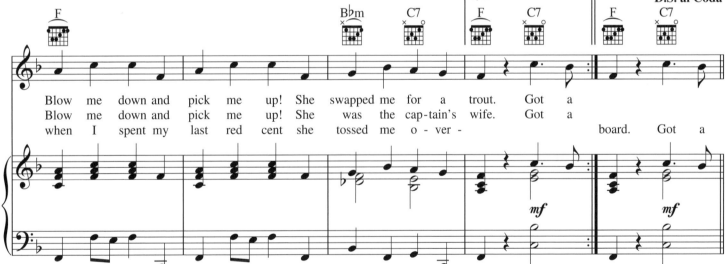

Blow me down and pick me up! She swapped me for a trout. Got a
Blow me down and pick me up! She was the cap-tain's wife. Got a
when I spent my last red cent she tossed me o - ver - board. Got a

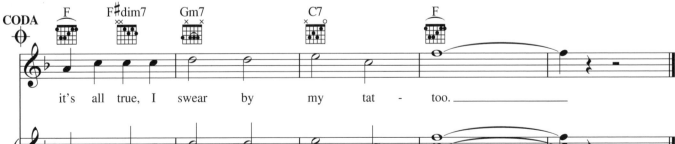

it's all true, I swear by my tat - too. _____

WONDER WOMAN

from the Warner Bros. TV Series WONDER WOMAN

Words by NORMAN GIMBEL
Music by CHARLES FOX

Moderately fast

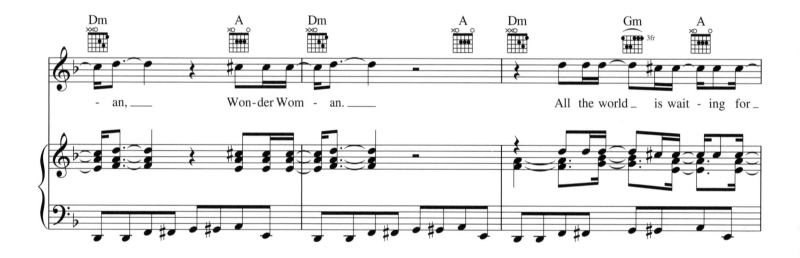

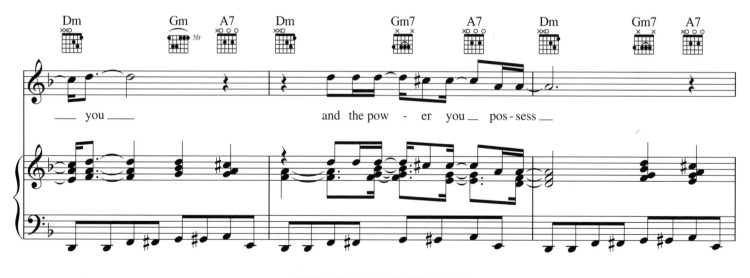

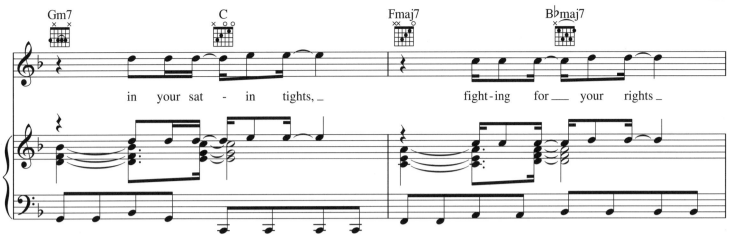

in your sat - in tights, _ fight-ing for _ your rights _

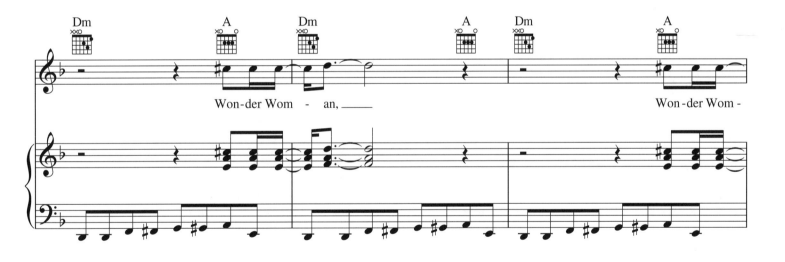

and the old _ Red, White _ and Blue. _____

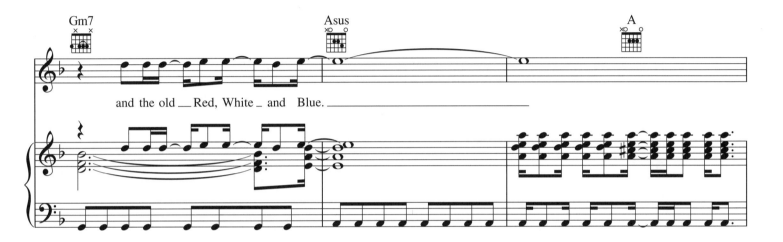

Won-der Wom - an, _____ Won-der Wom -

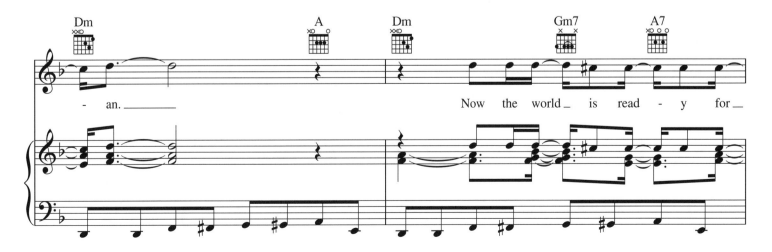

- an. _____ Now the world _ is read - y for _

you   and the won - ders you _ can do. _

Make a hawk _ a dove, _   stop a war _ with love, _   make a li - ar   tell the truth. _

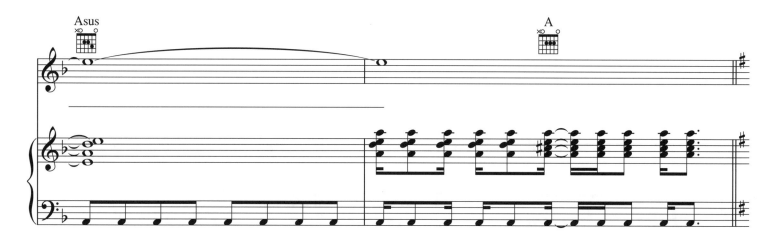

Won - der Wom - an _____

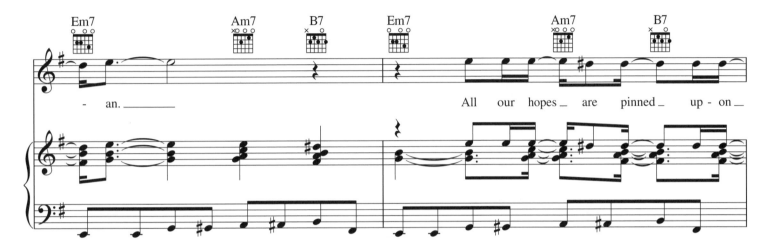

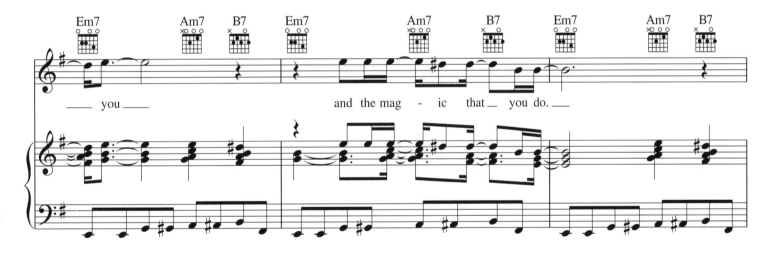

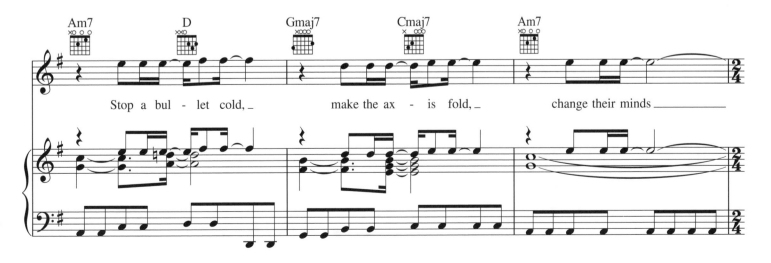

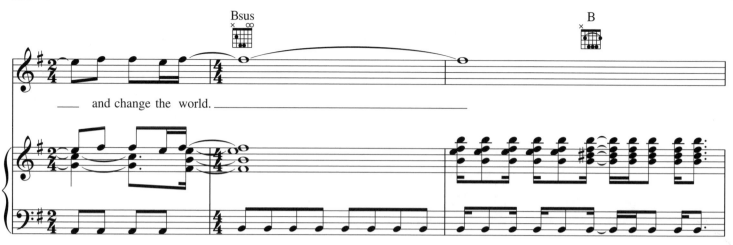

and change the world.

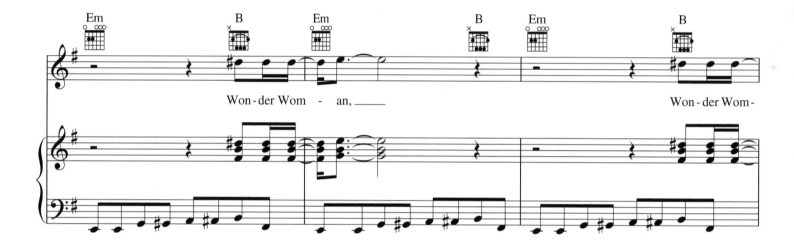

Won-der Wom - an, _____ Won - der Wom-

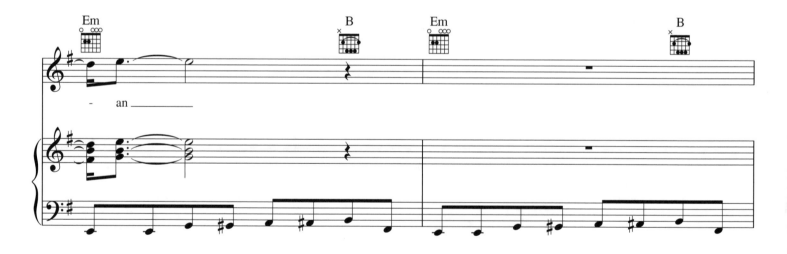

- an _____

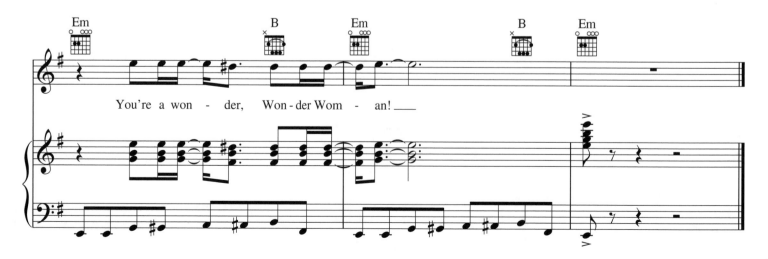

You're a won - der, Won - der Wom - an! _____